From the
Bottom of the
Barrel

Written by Pete White

This book is dedicated to the men and women of the Armed Forces who never made it home, to those who lost the battle with their demons and to everybody going through hell, keep going.

From the bottom of the barrel

DISCLAIMER: Let's get a few things out the way before we get going. I have written this book in a conversational style. I want it to come across as the genuine me, otherwise I'll come across as trying to be something that I'm not. I'm a bit of a gobshite, I have a filthy sense of humour and I love swearing. This brings me nicely to my next point, there will be swearing in this book. Again, because it's the authentic me but also swearing is a valuable tool in the English language for emphasising something. So, if swearing offends you then this may not be the right book for you.

Also, I'm not a trained writer and this is the first story I've ever told in a book, but I'm not shooting for any awards here; this is me telling a story that hopefully somebody will get some benefit from reading. Please take it for what it is, a story. I'm not writing war and peace here.

Oh, one more thing, at the start of every chapter I'm going to include one thing that I was told I can't do by one of my chain of command during the time I was suffering from severe mental health issues. This is either stuff I did, tried to do or asked if I could do. The idea has 3 aims:

Firstly, it shows what goes on in the mind of someone mentally ill.

Second, it adds a bit of light relief in a book that's going to get dark in places.

Lastly, it's just fucking funny looking back.

Acknowledgements

There are so many people who have had a huge impact on my life, to thank them all would require a book all on its own. So, I'll keep it to the core people who will see mentioned in this book. WARNING: Some of this is mega cheesy!

I want to start proceedings by thanking my amazing wife, Kelly. You are the brightest light in my life and through everything, the strongest and most unwavering support. No matter how bad things got (and they got pretty damn bad!) you've always been there, right by my side. I love and cherish you.

My family, there from the start and will be there until the end. You have always been a rock for me and a source of reassurance. I love you all.

Simo, A lot has changed over the years mate. We've gone from smashing back ungodly amounts of booze to full on family men, we may be more boring now, but one thing has never changed. You've always been there for me, no matter where I am in the world or how long I've been away you're a constant in my life. I can't thank you enough.

David (Paddy) Kivlehan and Paul (Twitch) Twitchwell, my friends, proof readers and subject matter experts. These guys have spent more time in the military than years I've been alive and have been a huge asset in getting this book completed and (hopefully) not shit. As a side note, Twitch is a motivational speaker and he's fucking brilliant, look him up at Veterans Mindset UK. Lastly, Paul Davies, the ridiculously talented photographer who helped me put together the cover design of this book. You can find him at www.bigwelshpaul.co.uk.

Chapter 1

Introduction

SAC White must not suggest using his genitals to fix broken kit or for anything other than their intended purpose

I've spent weeks thinking about whether I should write this book, thoughts like "I can barely string a sentence together, never mind write a whole book' and 'Nobody will give a shit about your story' kept flying through my mind. But after enough pestering from my wife and friends I decided to give it a go. Plus (for some reason), some people seem to like hearing about what's happened to me. But my main reason? Well this is an honest, upfront, no bullshit account of a bloke who suffered through severe mental health illness, through one of the shittiest times imaginable and came out the other side, not only alive but loving life and if this book can give one person going through a rough time a light at the end of the tunnel to focus on then surely, it's worth it, right?

I'm not much of a writer, like many people I've tried a few times through my life, each filled about 2 chapters and then I gave up, I guess the difference between then and now is that now I've actually got a story to tell. I never knew enough about one subject to write anything interesting about it or I've never had an attention span long enough to let my imagination create a piece of fiction that was any good. But what's to follow is 8 years of my life in which I started out by thinking I knew everything about life and myself. Quickly and painfully, I learnt that I knew fuck all about anything, and then built a brand new me. None of this 'New Year, new me' bullshit, it's more of a 'new life, new me'. I'm not aiming to write an autobiography, my life really isn't interesting enough for that, but what I aim to do is use my story to show people that no matter how bad things, get they will get better, maybe give some ideas for people on how to start turning things around and if it makes an interesting read for people in the process, well that's a bonus. Just be warned, there are points in this story where things will get dark, I intend for this to be a completely honest, nothing held back account of my journey through mental health because I believe that people aren't open enough about mental health. How can people feel safe to talk about their health issues if people still talk about mental health like they talk about sex toys? Mental health can be a very dark subject, but it can also make you do some pretty funny shit (such as printing out a photo of my Sergeants wife, make a paper cigar and display it in the office implying she's a post-op Winston Churchill) but more on this later.

As a result of everything that's happened to me, I've learned that the strongest people are those who have shed every ounce of pride and ego, let their façade fall and have been to the bottom of the barrel. When you've come from the bottom, you're a blank canvas and free to create whatever masterpiece you want. This is why whenever I hear someone say 'I suffered/suffer from mental health' I know they're strong, their own head has been their worst enemy and relentlessly beat the shit out of them, but they have fought back and they're still here which means they have won. To those still suffering, all I can say is keep going, keep fighting because you don't yet realise just how strong you are, you're a champion and although you may not be able to see the other side of that canvas, I promise you it's there.

This is the story of how I went from what my best mate described as "really bad diarrhoea shit" mental health issues where I was a genuinely horrible and, in some ways, a dangerous person to someone who loves life, is genuinely happy in themselves and runs a successful business helping other people to achieve their dream lives.

So why should you read the ramblings of an overweight 31-year-old Northerner? Well the fact that you're reading it means there's a good chance you've already paid for it, so you might as well. The main reason, however, is that not nearly enough people talk about mental health, and even if they do its usually pretty surface level or media friendly stuff. Nobody talks about the really shitty stuff. Hopefully, people will take something away from it, maybe it's a message of hope, maybe it's a lesson in fighting through adversity, it could be to learn a bit more about mental illness or maybe it's that feeling when you're at the train station looking at people and thinking 'what's their story?' Well here's mine.

Chapter 2

Young, dumb and full of hope

SAC White must not publicly point out the flaws in his chain of command, even if he is right.

I guess you could say my journey started on the 9th of February 2009. At 8am to be exact. That was the moment I officially joined the Royal Air Force. I was 21 at the time. At this point if you're now thinking 'Wait a minute, you've just skipped 21 years?' Well there's two reasons for that. For a start I had a very unsexy upbringing, 2 parents who worked their arses off, my mam was a Nurse with the NHS for nearly 40 years, my dad is disabled and was a factory worker until he was made redundant before spending a few years in retail. One sister who's considerably smarter than me and works in finance and a happy home life. Me and my sister were never left wanting for anything because my folks worked incredibly hard and were smart with their money. They never moaned about it, they just got on with it. Secondly, something I only learnt a week before I began writing this book is while it's fairly common knowledge that Post Traumatic Stress Disorder (PTSD) has a habit of pushing all those shitty memories to some dark recess in your mind, it also takes other, completely normal memories with it so I really don't remember huge chunks of my childhood or I have vastly distorted memories of that time of my life. It's pretty shitty but I'm working on restoring those memories. Anyway, I was embarking on what I thought would be a lifelong career as an engineer in the RAF. It was something I'd always wanted to do since I was a kid and now, I was doing it. When I first visited the Armed Forces Careers Office, I wanted to join the infantry, I wanted to shoot stuff, throw grenades, play soldier, look cool and live the call of duty dream. The Sergeant behind the army desk was on his last week before he left the forces and didn't give a shit about recruiting anyone who would be better off doing something else. Because of this, he told me I was wasting my time since I had good GCSE's and should get a skill (I would apologise to the Infantry lads but they're probably too busy finding out if different coloured Crayons have different flavours). I went away, looked at the options and decided to become a Communications Engineer in the Royal Air Force. It wasn't glamorous, it wasn't sexy, but I was always a bit of a geek growing up and the recruiter told me I could fly drones if I enlisted into that job (lying bastard!). Over the next 6 months, while my application went through processing and assessment, I spent my time training to get fitter. I was a weedy computer geek who spent most of his spare time playing computer games and avoiding any kind of sport. I did a pretty good job of getting fit considering I had no knowledge of it. I'd smash out as many press-ups and sit ups as I could a few times a day, I started running and going to the gym, I had no idea what I was doing but figured if I kept swearing and lifting heavy stuff it would work. I was kind of right.

On the morning of the 9th Feb 2009 I got on the train and travelled from Teesside down to RAF Halton for my basic training, It was my first time using the London underground and I was travelling in a suit with 2 large ruck sacks, an ironing board and a laptop bag, imagine a sweaty mess in a shirt and tie, carrying all this shit while running through the tube station (because I didn't know the underground trains ran every couple of minutes). It's not an experience I'll be in a hurry to repeat.

I turned up at basic training on a mini bus imagining something like the US Marine recruits you see on TV, shouting screaming and being called a maggot. It really wasn't anything like that, providing you shut up, did what you are told and did it quickly it was fine. Maybe it would be more of a shock to a young 16-year-old scrote (and I did see a few of them in tears or leaving after a couple of days) but at 21 I had a little more life experience behind me (not much, just a bit). Basic training in the RAF is pretty tame compared to the other UK armed forces, it's more mind games as opposed just getting constantly beasted until your eye balls bleed (for our civilian friends out there, a beasting is getting thrashed with continuous, exhausting exercise, usually used as a punishment for whatever you did wrong, it sucks balls but it'll get you seriously fit). My reasoning was; the sooner you come to terms with the fact that nothing you do will be good enough then the easier it gets. It's just a big game and your instructors perform a well-rehearsed act. Whenever they were shouting and screaming and making you feel like a piece of shit,

I always thought to myself 'Your finger has poked through the toilet paper and into your arsehole just like everyone else'. Providing I avoided the urge to piss myself laughing at this thought it helped to humanise them. This is a technique I still use to this day when I speak to highly successful or imposing people. Acknowledge that at some point everyone has got an unintentional shitty finger, and nobody will intimidate you again. I intentionally kept my head down and made myself the grey man letting the bigger personalities get the shit from the instructors. Usually the gobshites giving it the big-I-am on the flight would find themselves out in front doing press ups or sprinting around the parade square.

5 weeks in to my 9-week training and my plans were put on hold when I developed shin splints which made anything more than a gentle walk agony. Shin splints are pretty common in basic training because people, like myself, haven't prepared their bodies for the physical exertion you get in basic training. In the RAF when you can't meet one of the training criteria because you're either injured or just had a shitty day and didn't pass whatever test for you, you're taken away from your training fight and put on one of two other flights. One Flight, who I knew as the 'fuck up flight', is for the people who failed a test or failed to meet the minimum training criteria, they get remedial training and are usually quickly put back into mainstream training with a new intake of trainees. The other flight is for all those who

get injured, these ranged from serious back injuries or broken bones to relatively minor stuff like shin splints. There were always a few people who just couldn't be arsed to do the physical exercise. The trainees in this flight are put through some kind of physio and a tailored fitness programme designed to get them fit again. A few will never be well enough to return to training, so they're sent packing. I was in the second flight and this was a complete change of pace to normal training, I spent 4 months on that flight doing 2 lots of phys (physical training sessions) every day and spent large chunks of time sitting around doing nothing. After the 4 months I still wasn't fully fit. But being on this injury flight was shit, I was bored and some of the personalities on there were just constant victims of their own actions; they pissed me off and I wanted to get away from them. So, I made out that I was fully fit and was allowed back to mainstream training. Because it had been so long, I had to start my basic training again from day 1 again but this time round it was easy, I knew and understood the game and how to play it, this time round I naturally found myself in a leader role within my new flight. The new lads looked to me as someone who could help them with the new skills they had to learn like ironing, making the bed and getting their shit together (seriously, it was a miracle some of these guys could tie their own shoe laces). The training staff are usually happy for someone to take the role of leader amongst the lads. They let me crack on and I enjoyed the new responsibility. The next 9 weeks passed by smoothly; we only lost a couple of lads from training through injury or finding out that it wasn't for them and I graduated from basic training in November 2009.

Despite feeling proud that I'd finally passed out and couldn't wait to for my mam and dad to come watch me graduate, my graduation parade was shit. The military band failed to turn up so rather than marching with the traditional military music, we marched in total silence, only a faint 'left, right left' could be heard as some of the lads and lasses whispered the cadence. We were meant to get a Tornado fast jet doing a fly past, instead we got some shitty little aircraft flown by one of the brothers of the graduating lads. Still, it was great to have this first chapter of my career under my belt and I could move on

Chapter 3

A rock and a hard place

SAC White must not use 'Its fucked' to diagnose broken
equipment on technical forms

This is going to be a short chapter because, well, let's call
it for what it is, it's fucking boring. But I can't just skip
an entire year of my 9 years in the RAF. So, after I left
basic training, I went onto RAF Cosford near
Wolverhampton, this is basically one big training base
for technical trades in the RAF. When applying to join
the RAF I chose to join as a comms engineer. I'd always
been good with computers as a kid and it meant getting
some decent qualifications rather than spending an entire
career in the military and leaving with nothing useful in
civvy street. Training for my trade was 12 months, loads
of maths, radar theory, learning how satellites work and
IT geek stuff; nothing glamorous, sexy or particularly
interesting for a book. I found training tough going
because it was all pretty academic stuff and I've never
been one for academics. I always liked making and
breaking stuff and I thought homework was a waste of
time as far as I was concerned. I failed more than one
exam there and had to retake it later on.

I trained with 12 other lads and lasses; we lived together,
worked together, got pissed together and argued
together. There were even a couple of fights thrown in
there for good measure. At the time, we all grew fairly
close and got to know each other well but I think most

of us have lost touch as time has done on and I think only one of them is still in the military at the time of writing.

It was during this time I met my future wife and with that being the case now feels the best time to introduce her, especially as she was to become the corner stone of my life and one of the major reasons that I'm still here, also you'll be hearing about her quite a bit through this book. Me and Kelly first met in 2008 on a cruise ship going around the Canary Islands. On a ship full of people who would have been considered young back in the 50s seeing her meant that I had someone a similar age to me to spend time with. On the face of it, we couldn't have been much more different. I was an outdoor pursuits instructor, good with my hands but shit with anything academic. Kel was a person centred counsellor, had a degree and spent her working life sitting down and talking to people. Despite our differences we hit it off straight away, we spent every day of the holiday together. I didn't feel any of the awkwardness you usually do when first meeting a fit lass. At the time, it was a holiday romance and not much else, at least to me anyway. She fell for me pretty hard, but I was a bit of a selfish wanker back then and fancied playing the field, so I told her I wasn't interested in a relationship. Apart from a single visit later in the year we didn't really talk again until I finished with my previous girlfriend (a gold digging, nightmare banshee (hey it's my book, I'm allowed to be a little bitchy). After I finished with her, Kel and I started seeing each other, 3 years later we got married. I could talk all day about her and

I'm not afraid to get all cheesy about her because she's fucking amazing but most of it would be irrelevant to the story, all you need to know at this point is that she's put up with me at my very worst, acting like a total cock, and stuck by me throughout.

Anyway, back to the phase 2 training, there's not much more to tell. 20 odd essays, a shit load of exams and parades later and I graduated 12 months later. I never really had any issues in my phase 2 training and was looking forward to getting going with my career, I was keen to get started and although this part was a pain in the arse it was a necessary pain in the arse to get me where I wanted to be. All you need to know is I trained as a Communications Engineer and my wife is fucking quality, that's all you really need to take away from this chapter.

Chapter 4

FNG

SAC White must not suggest that my ginger colleague do
the more dangerous jobs because he has no soul

After graduating from phase 2 training I went on to my
first posting at RAF Leeming in North Yorkshire in
November 2010, it is a flying base but not much flies
from there; fast jet pilots in training fly their Hawk jets
from there but that's about it except for the odd
Typhoon fast jet stopping overnight. The biggest
contingent of people at Leeming is at the Tactical
Comms Wing (TCW). The role of TCW is to deploy
with whatever communications platforms are required,
usually to shitty areas of the world. They set up their kit
so everyone else can have working phones, computers
and ensure that the UK can communicate with wherever
there are troops deployed. If my memory is right (which
its's usually not these days), they were the most deployed
unit during the entire Afghanistan war because they were
the only unit of its type in the RAF and as a result, were
constantly rotating troops for the entire conflict. Sounds
a bit sexier than the last chapter doesn't it? Well, here's
the thing; with the exception of a few units, most of the
military spend months and months of doing nothing,
absolutely fuck all going on with briefs periods of being
busy or doing something worthwhile. It can be soul
destroying sometimes. Here's the other thing, civilians
tend to imagine the military as this close-knit band of

brother's type of thing. When it comes to the RAF, that's a load of bullshit and here's why; when the guys finish work, they head back to the accommodation block, lock their door and spend their time on whatever games console they've got. People will step on their own gran to get promoted, there's a lot of cliques and bitching and what a lot of people call banter, is actually just acting like a bit of a dick. Lastly the chain of command (CoC) just couldn't care less about the welfare of the guys working under them, this is displayed as them being anything from just being a bit of a dick to full on negligence. More on this later.

My first day on my new unit I was shitting myself. When you graduate from basic and phase 2 training you leave there as the top of the pile, you're the mutts nuts, you know the game and you know how to play it. You're full of pride because you've passed everything they've thrown at you and the whole graduation process is designed to make you feel proud. Then all of a sudden, you're bottom of the pile again, nobody knows who you are and most people don't give a shit. So, I turned up to the front reception of TCW with the rest of the new guys (oh and in case you're wondering FNG stands for 'Fucking New Guy'), a few of them were guys I trained with. We stood by the stairs in a row and waited, one by one each of the 4 squadrons Warrant Officers came down the stairs and picked out the number of new guys they had been allocated by the higher ups, it felt like being chosen for football teams in school. The first of us went onto 4 Squadron, the Warrant Officer from there was entirely forgettable, the next 3 went onto 1

Squadron, again completely forgettable. With 3 of us left there the Warrant Officer from 2 Squadron came down the stairs, you could hear him coming long before you saw him. A short, loud Irish bloke. He reminded me of a chihuahua, makes a lot of noise but wouldn't break a grape in a fruit fight. He told the two stood next to me they were his. He then told them that they were to write a 'pen picture' (basically a life story) and have it on his desk by the start of the next day. What a twat. Like when I played football in school, I was the last one to be picked. My Warrant Officer from 3 squadron was a tall, grey haired, balding bloke with glasses, he was soft spoken and seemed like a decent bloke. Every Squadron is broken down into 2 flights, he told me which flight I was on and showed me to the office where I'd be working. This was a long room filled with bored looking people sat in office chairs chatting; of course, as soon as I walked in a lot of the conversations stopped while they assessed the FNG, quickly made their first impressions and went back to chatting. I found a chair, sat down and waited for something to happen. After a few days of this I got bored and decided to try a different tact, I walked in to the office, picked one of the biggest cliques in the office, pulled up a chair, sat in the middle of them and tried to spark up a conversation with them. These were effectively the 'popular' kids on the flight, so this was the social equivalent of taking a shit on the floor and jumping into the pile with all my force making sure everyone got at least one freckle of shit on their face. This it made me as popular as a hand grenade missing the pin. Oops.

The next few months consisted of hearing various bits of random bullshit about myself, being spoken to like shit by the some of the guys I worked with and desperately trying to find work to keep myself busy, I even took it upon myself to organise the stationery cupboard which lead to me being awarded the position of 'IC stationery' (IC meaning 'In Charge' in military lingo), a position that nobody wanted, including myself and meant I ordered new pens and pencils from central stores, apparently this helped my chances of promotion; what a croc of shit, but it gave me something to do for a couple of hours a week. Eventually, I just allowed the incoming shit from others to roll off me; of course, some of it did get to me on some level but I never let it show. I remember going for lots of extended shits in the disabled toilet just to get out of the office for a bit and to play games on my phone without getting a bollocking. This nicely sums up the military in one sentence.

This was a far cry from what I pictured when I first joined up, sat in an office, bored off my tits with the highlight of my day ordering replacement pens. It wasn't exactly what the recruiters promises. The more experienced guys on the Squadron had more of the work, they would have routine maintenance on the comms equipment or would be testing a new method or bit of kit. I usually volunteered to help out but often this would be refused by the CoC for some unknown reason or the guys doing the job didn't want some new guy getting in the way. Every few months the Squadron would go on ex (exercise); driving to the arse end of nowhere, somehow always managing to pick the days with the worst weather. Ex was a relief from the monotony of the office and a chance to at least act like we were in the military, even if it did mean getting thrashed about in a field for a couple of weeks in the freezing cold Yorkshire Moors with only a hip flask and a photo of Kel to keep me warm.

Chapter 5

We're all going on a summer holiday

SAC White must not perform a strip tease while in work.
Even if it is a birthday present for one of the lads

Because each of the 4 Squadrons rotate deployments
every 4 months It was common knowledge that we were
deploying to Afghanistan in April 2011 but there are
always a handful of people left behind to keep things
running back on base. They also acted as replacements if
anyone got hurt and had to be shipped back home, they
would also keep the families of those deployed happy, I
assumed I would be one of them, as one of the new
guys. By some stroke of luck or managerial fuck up; I
was pulled into the office by my Sergeant and told that I
would be deploying with the squadron in April 2011. I
was over the moon with this, I wanted to join the
military to travel to different places and have new
experiences and it be a chance for me to do the job I
joined up to do and hopefully a worthwhile job that
would make a difference. Up until this point the military
had completely failed to live up to my expectations, I
was a glorified office worker in uniform and was
seriously regretting my choice to join the RAF instead of
the Army.

Kel was less keen, in fact she was devastated when I told
her, it's always difficult to explain to loved ones why you
want to go to a war zone but at the same time she knew
that it would happen one day, I just don't think she

expected it to happen within 6 months of me joining the Squadron. I was fucking ecstatic and my excitement to deploy made Kel feel like she had to accept it for my sake; that, and a shit load of reassurance that I wouldn't be doing any fighting, in fact if someone in my job had to shoot at anyone then something had seriously gone tits up. (Spoiler alert: If you're reading this hoping for war stories about me running through enemy fire to rescue an injured comrade or abseiling down a building dressed in black then I've got bad news for you, I was a comms techy in the RAF. Nothing like that ever happened)

Eventually I found out that my job would be as a technician on a widely used secret computer system. This suited me perfectly, it was a small role, but it was role non-the-less and I'd get to experience working in a war zone. In the lead up to our deployment everyone had various courses to do aimed to help them do whatever job they were assigned. I went on a 3-week course to learn about the system I would be working on, I won't go into details about it, not because it's a big secret (though there probably are parts of it that are secretive) but because if I found it mind numbingly dull learning it; me telling you about it would be soul destroying...for you.

A few weeks before we deployed, we started pre-deployment training. This was stuff like learning patrol techniques, landmine detection, vehicle and people search drills and contact drills both on foot and in a vehicle (contact being a military term for getting shot at).

It was fun playing soldier but none of this is stuff that any of us would ever do, to the guys who go outside the wire and do the soldiering we were what was known was REMFs (Rear Echelon Mother fuckers), meaning we never really left the safety of the base and supported the guys who did go out and do that stuff. But the CoC needed to get those boxes ticked and it was fun, so we made the most of the experience. We spent one day learning how to profile individuals to work out whether they were a threat, if they could be wearing a suicide vest, if they were gathering intel on us (known as 'dicking', because they were dicks) and how to judge your local surroundings to look for clues of an attack. This really stuck with me for some reason and it's something I still sometimes find myself doing now, even though the chance of an ambush or IED happening in Shropshire are slightly lower than in Afghanistan. On one occasion I remember we were doing patrol and contact drills on foot, the bad guys (played by some of the more experienced lads) opened fire with blank rounds, one of our lads was declared as injured. In typical fashion myself and one other were ordered to drag the casualty out of the contact. We had to drag the guy who probably weighed 160 pounds, plus his weapon, body armour, load carrying kit and spare ammunition a couple of hundred yards over this field while carrying all your own shit. I've never been a particularly fit bloke but even for someone who's really fit, this is a balls to the wall job and pretty quickly you find yourself hanging out of your arse, I struggled big time. This was when I first had the idea that the whole image of playing soldier wasn't what the video games and movies promised it would be.

Me and Kel had been together for over a year by this point. I'd always been a bit of a twat when it came to the ladies and (true to form) in the early days of me and her I messed Kel about a bit. I was seeing somebody else at the same time as her, telling her I wasn't interested in anything serious etc (I even called her the other girls name at one point (lads, trust me, don't do it!)). But she stuck with me and made an honest fella out of me, I felt like I'd be a total knob if I didn't do right by her and couldn't really see a future in which I wouldn't settle down with her. I decided that I'd get things cemented down and propose to her, I was a true gent and asked her folks for permission (her mam was over the moon, her dad said "Do whatever you got to do"). So, a couple of weeks before I left for Afghan, we went on holiday to spend some quality time together, I proposed to her in bed. I shit you not, the amount that she cried I genuinely thought I'd seriously fucked something up! But yeah, all was good, she said yes, and there was the added bonus of shopping around for wedding stuff would keep her busy while I was away.

During the final stages of the build-up to deployment we each had to get an individual photo taken in uniform, the format of the photo was very specific, well pressed camouflage shirt and stood at an angle in front of one of our green trucks. At first nobody said why we were getting this done, some kind of media release?
Eventually I asked one of the guys who had deployed

before, he told me these were the pictures that would be sent to the news agencies if we were killed on tour so they could show it on the news. This took me back a bit, we're all RAF comms techies, we don't do shit that would get us killed. The next part seemed even more drastic, we were each given a form to complete, this form asked for very specific details about ourselves, our mother's maiden name, hair colour, eye colour, blah blah blah. The last box asked us to write a short story from our lives containing specific details. The idea of this form is that if we were taken hostage by the bad guys these details would be used by the Special Forces lads to identify us in a rescue attempt. Here's the story I used (with some name changes):

"In year 9 at St Rodney's school where we had to learn wedding vows in religious education class. While reading it out to the class I said "I Pete White, do take thee, my right hand, to be my lawfully wedded wife". Miss James threw me out of the class and told me I would never pass any of my GCSE's acting like that. I told her that she would never find a husband with a personality like that".

I got 10 decent GCSE's by the way; screw you Miss James!

Chapter 6

A windy, sandy, shit hole

My sergeant is not undercover Spetznas and he didn't
cause the Chernobyl incident

Early in the morning, sometime in April 2011 around 70
of us with 4 months' worth of kit were met by a couple
of buses on base. It's impressive how much you can fit
into a black holdall and a Bergen. I remember seeing a
bunch of our guys, normally hard arse bloke types who
would consider any form of emotion a weakness saying
emotional goodbyes to their other halves, it made the
whole thing seem more real to me, this shit was really
happening. I'd said my goodbyes to Kel a few days
before while I was on leave at my parents, I won't lie, I
shed a tear at the time, it was tough, and I knew that Kel
couldn't get past the newspaper headlines about lads and
lasses getting killed over there. It didn't matter to her
that my job wouldn't be a dangerous one and I was
unlikely to be in any immediate danger. If the shit hit the
fan there would be a literal army of people, there to step
in and deal with it. But explaining this to a civvy was
difficult and in Kels mind Afghanistan equals danger, So,
she was in bits. We said our goodbyes on the doorstep,
and she drove back to Birmingham (yeah, I fell for a
Brummie, she must be a good egg for me to put up with
that accent!).

We loaded up our kit and were driven up to the local
civilian airport, from there we took a flight to RAF Brize

Norton, then from Brize to Dubai where I thought we'd stop for a quick refuel and move on, but we had a 24 hour wait for the next flight in the 'departures lounge'. In reality this was a single thin-skinned building with a few camping chairs and tables and some brew making equipment. That was so fucking dull, most of us had left our mobiles at home for security reasons (the sneaky bastard bad guys have a habit of using phone signals to triangulate targets for mortar and rocket strikes). I don't remember much of this part, just loads of waiting around in a very hot tent.

Eventually we jumped on a Hercules and flew into Camp Bastion. The insurgents have a habit of taking pot shots at incoming aircraft, so transport flights would usually land in theatre at night. As we had loads of large kit inside the aircraft with us, we were all sat down the sides of the aircraft in between the kit, effectively flying sideways. When it came to landing, we all put on our body armour and helmets, the lights were turned off, so we were sat in pitch black. If things didn't feel real already, they sure as hell did now. Whereas civilian flights tend to take a long and gradual descent on the approach to the runway, military flights flying into hostile environments take a much steeper and faster descent to the runway. This was a fucking weird sensation, sat sideways, leaning at a 45-degree angle, in the pitch black and in body armour. I wouldn't say that I felt scared at this point, but I was apprehensive and unsure what to expect. It was like the first day in a new job, but nobody is sure what the job actually is yet and with people who want to kill you all over the place.

When anyone first arrives in theatre (regardless of if they have been there before or not) they spend a few days on RSOI which stands for Reception, Staging, Onward movement and integration this is basically a military way of saying 'get your shit together, get used to the place before you start your job. It's like an induction at work with more sand and guns, unless you managed to find a beach in Manchester, then probably the same amount of sand and guns (I'm taking the piss before anyone threatens to sue!). For us it consisted of shit loads of briefs about how things run, what we're up to, what the Jinglys were up to (Let's get this bit out the way now. Jingly refers to the trucks driven in Afghan, they were decorated with chains and bells that jingle as they drove along the non-existent roads. The locals driving them are therefore called Jinglys and was eventually adopted to all of the locals. I don't know whether it's offensive or not, I don't use it to be offensive, it's just how I know them and quicker than saying local national). Anyway, we also spent some time on the range zeroing our rifles and getting familiarised with the base. This wasn't quick as Bastion was fucking huge, over 30,000 people staying in a camp the size of Reading. This feels like a good point in the story for a bit of a tangent and explain Bastion a bit more as it will feature heavily later on.

Camp Bastion was a British base positioned towards the North of Helmand province and at its peak was made up of a few different areas. There was the main British camp made up of a shit load of troop accommodation, supply areas, runways, transport, welfare areas for internet and calls home. We even had a pizza hut and

KFC serving out of converted shipping containers, though to eat there you were taking your life and the health of your arse hole in your hands. There were a bunch of shops, ran by each of the nations based there (Brits, Yanks, Danish, Dutch etc). There were also shops and market stalls ran by Jinglys, with everything from barbers to shops selling knock off military kit and Velcro patches for your kit. These jingly shops were usually a bit shit, typically selling a half-arsed fake product or service. You could even pick up a Rolex for $10. I never had anything against the guys running them, most of them (as far as I know) were just innocent civvys just trying to make a living. Getting a haircut from them would usually result in you looking like you'd had a fight with a lawn mower.

Our accommodation ranged from decent 2 story hard skinned accommodation with air con and proper beds, this was usually used by civvy contractors. There were the pods which looked like inflated tents, they were modular, so they'd strap a bunch of them together and create mega tents with their own corridors and toilets. Then there were the shite 8-man tents left over from the cold war, these were air conditioned (when it worked) and had 8 mini mosquito net pods each, 1 for each person. The beds were camp cot which were fucking awful but compared to what the guys out in the forward operating bases (FOBs) and Patrol bases (PBs) what we had was luxury. We had toilet and shower blocks which were like what you see at festivals; most of the toilets were port-a-loo style things. We used to call them sweat boxes because you'd sweat your tits off with the sun beating down on it while trying to take a shit in them.

Bastion also had a large contingent of US marines who stopped in Camp Leatherneck, their accommodation was ace, they had small semi-permanent buildings with only 2-4 guys stopping in it, they had TV's, sofa's, and even had BBQ's. Their food was also gorgeous, and they had a top-notch gym; jammy bastards. Camp Shorabak was the compound for the Afghan Army and Police. I never went in this bit because I never needed to or wanted to; it always gave me an uneasy feeling. They slept there, ate there, trained there and rarely ventured out unless they were going on an op. The rest of the camp was mostly logistics, support, massive helipad and runways. It even had its own dedicated IT support 'company' made up of 3 shitty tents sewn together. There's plenty of videos on YouTube showing Camp Bastion if you want to get a feel for it.

Anyway, where were we? Oh yeah RSOI. So yeah, we stopped there for 3 days; the guys who were there to do stuff at the pointy end of things stopped longer for more area specific training. Of the approx. 70 of us who flew over there I think 15 or so stopped there to help out with the comms stuff in Bastion; the rest of us jumped on a plane and flew over to Kandahar.

Chapter 7

Butlins with bombs

SAC White must not spank himself with network cables
whilst pretending to be a porn star and demanding he be
called 'Luna Lovegood'

We landed at Kandahar in another Hercules at around
11pm, by this point we were all knackered and just
wanted to crawl into our pits and get some sleep. We
had to jump on a bus which would take us to our
accommodation, but this was a bus journey the likes of
which I've never known. This thing would have been
considered new in the 70s, every single inch of it was
covered in sand and dust, what was left of the air con
just blew warm dust around the bus. The driver was
clearly at the point of 'I don't care what happens to me,
this bus or the guys on it'. This was probably because he
was scared shitless the Taliban would find out he was
working for the enemy. The last time the bus passed any
kind of road worthiness inspection I was still in nappies.
If I wasn't too tired to care I would have been shitting
myself about us driving in pitch black with barely
working headlights on roads that resembled what I
imagine the surface of the moon looks like.

Our accommodation was 5* compared to Bastion, more
like barrack blocks from our training days. Long
buildings with 4-man rooms either side. Every room has
2 bunk beds, bed side tables, wardrobes and most of
them had a TV left over by the previous guys. We even

had proper showers and toilets and decent air con. Although I always felt like it was a bit of a piss take on the guys who got the shitty end of the stick when it came to their accommodation, I was glad to have the comfort.

This pretty much sums up Kandahar. It was run by the Americans and the Canadians so everything there was just bigger and better than Bastion. While Bastion was basically tent city, Kandahar was closer to a normal city. Buildings were purpose build, well equipped. There were Gym's dotted all over the place and there was a shopping centre full of shops from all the different nations based there. It even had a TGI Fridays, a Timmy Hortons (which was a fucking god send thanks to their amazing brews and doughnuts) and a kebab shop. Kandahar was primarily an airbase, even before we got there the Afghans had Kandahar international airport which the yanks built in the 50s as a civilian airport but barely got used. The soviets took it over in the 80s and used it for military aircraft, after they left it fell into rag order until the Canadians and Aussies turned up in 2001 and made it the starting point for what Kandahar airport would later become, basically a sprawling military mini city. I used to think of it as some kind of holiday camp but in a war zone, a sort of Butlins resort but with more bombs.

Anyway, my second night there I got my first little taste of a war zone. I was lying on my bed, wasting time on my laptop when the IDF alarm sounded. IDF stands for Indirect fire. This means they're chucking rockets and mortars in your general direction. In our information briefs before and after we got into theatre, we were told all about this and what we should do but like everything else it never seemed real so when I heard this alarm, I had the following thought process;

"Is that a drill? Well its 9pm so I doubt it, oh, this is actually happening? Ah shit ok then, Should I be shitting myself? I'm not sure. Balls, guess I should get down then"

I put on my helmet and body armour and sat on the floor and waited to see what happened. After 30 seconds or so I heard a bang in the distance, and that was it. I was wearing this bastard gear, sitting on the bastard floor for the equivalent of a bastard distant firework. Turns out that IDF is pretty much a daily occurrence in Kandahar. They were launched from within the mountains next to the base and most of the time they overshoot, missing completely. A few would land within the base but rarely cause much damage. They had a habit of hitting poo pond which isn't a euphemism. It's literally a pond of poo, it's where all the camps shit and piss goes. Seeing the area surround poo pond splattered with shite became a regular occurrence. In the early days, every time we had IDF, I would put on my body armour and helmet and get on the floor; after a couple of weeks I chilled out about it and just on my helmet (since my body armour was useless, no really, it was completely useless) and get on the floor. Eventually that turned into just my helmet; after a couple of weeks if it went off during the night I'd just stay in my bed because I figured that if one of them hit my building there's not a damn thing the helmet, body armour or sitting on the floor was going to do for me.

My job in Kandahar was pretty basic. I was a member of a 4-man team looking after a secret computer system which wasn't particularly widely used. Every day we had a few tasks to carry out like making sure backups ran and keeping dust out of the kit but other than that it was responding to stuff breaking down which didn't happen much. Because of this we spent a lot of time sitting around with nothing to do. I used to get told off by my Corporal for playing solitaire in the office, so I started volunteering to do the equipment maintenance, taking the laptop with me and taking a suspiciously long time to finish the work and becoming strangely talented at card games. Sometimes I'd pass the time by making work for myself; I created a spreadsheet which would use formulas to calculate how many minutes, hours, days and weeks you had left in theatre. Every day would have a different picture of women wearing next to nothing. The concept was nothing new, they're called 'Chuff' charts and are widely used, but I just fancied making my own. I tried my hand at making scripts that would test the network automatically, they worked well but the powers that be weren't interested in anything that would make even less work for folks. This place was run like a corporate office, full of work place politics and bullshit, it drove me nuts. The problem is, if I didn't find something productive to do, I'd end up getting myself in trouble. One-night shift I got bored and found myself looking at the weapons rack in the office. By this point I'd never had any pistol training, so they were still a novelty to me. I started playing with a Sig Sauer pistol (because playing with guns is always a good idea). I pulled the slide back on the gun and revelled in how it made me feel like some kind of action hero, a short, podgy action hero; like a low budget Jason Statham after a few hundred kebabs and pies. I quickly realised that I couldn't get the slide forwards again, I pressed every button and slide I could find (except the trigger) but couldn't get it back to its original position. They say crisis is the mother of all invention, well, not in this case, I went into full cluster fuck mode. I put the pistol back in the weapons rack and walked away like nothing had happened. After I sat down at my desk, one of the more senior lads on the Squadron waited a few minutes before announcing that he was doing a 'weapons check', he individually expected each of the rifles and pistols in the weapons rack before coming across the pistol I'd been fucking around with. He asked each person in the office if they had been playing with the guns, everyone (including me) said no. He said that the pistol was issued to our commanding officer and that it was broken and that he'd need to report this to the chain of command for investigation. I spent the next few days shitting myself waiting to get an almighty bollocking. What I didn't know is that one this lad had been watching me the whole time, there was no such thing as a 'weapons check (at least not in that sense) and he was fucking with me.

This taught me two things:

> 1.   I'm a fucking terrible liar. Every time I've tried to get away with lying, I've been caught out, that's why I'm always honest now, no matter what the consequences. Even if I have to tell the Mrs she looks awful in that dress.
>
> 2.   I need to keep myself busy or I get myself in trouble.

Things move pretty slow in a war zone. It's long periods of nothing followed by short periods of things going bat shit crazy. I was bored and felt like I wasn't making any kind of difference being there. I continually asked my Sergeant if there was any extra work on; you know how they say be careful what you wish for? Well, 3 weeks into my tour and myself and 3 others were called into the office and told that the guys at Camp Bastion had loads of work and needed some extra man power, so we were going to be sent over there. All 4 of us were gutted, we were going to be leaving the holiday camp in a war zone for a ghetto in a war zone (at least as far as I was concerned, the RAF isn't exactly knowing for slumming it, the guys out in the FOB's and PB's really did have it tough). One of the lads in our newly shit on group of lads managed to wriggle his way out of it and stay but the 3 of us who remained were stuck on a Herc and flew over to Bastion a couple of days later.

Chapter 8

A hot, windy, sandy shit hole

'I'm drunk' is a bad response to any question asked by any officer

Whenever people ask me "What was Afghanistan like?" my reply is usually "A hot, windy, sandy shit hole" because the first place that comes to mind is Bastion and that's exactly what this place was. Zero visibility sand storms were pretty common, dust devils (like mini twisters) would fly over your head and sand blast your face and it was fucking 54°C. No, really, this place gets stupidly hot in the summer and stupidly cold in the winter. It's basically the worst place on the planet, with the worst climate and some of the worst people. It's a real shit hole.

We got to Bastion and found our way to the Comms Section, the Army Staff Sergeant in charge (a scary looking bastard with a perfectly square head and buzz cut who looked like he loathed little scrotes like me) was surprised to see us and didn't know why we'd been sent. The wankers back in Kandahar had sent us to get us out of the way because they didn't have anything for us to do. Rather than send us back again the guys in Bastion decided to try and find jobs for us to do.

The first lad got a job working on the service desk, this was basically an IT call centre in the desert. There were 3 lads doing the work of 10. It was good, honest work but fucking brutal, the shifts were long and workload was insane. I was unspeakably relieved not to be shafted with this one. The second lad landed a seriously cushy gig working with the US marines, he was basically an IT dogs' body, fixing shit, setting shit up and doing whatever was needed. The job was easy, he had one of those Gucci American rooms I told you about earlier with access to the best food and gym in the camp. That left me, there was talk of me doing one of the jobs above, but nobody had space, it looked like I was going to be doing fuck all again. Suddenly they found a job for me working at JFCIS (A) which stands for Joint Forces Communications Information Systems (Afghanistan), basically it was the headquarters for comms across Afghan and back to the UK. Full of officers and with important stuff going on, result!

I was told I'd be working as a Comms Watchman on nights. My job would be to monitor one of the 6 massive TVs which would display any issues with the various communications networks across all British bases in Afghan. The building was like an aircraft hangar converted into a huge open plan office. Rows and rows of desks, each with an officer specializing in a different aspect of the war. Everyone would clear off by 11pm, leaving me on my own to keep an eye on things. If anything went wrong, I'd call the civvy contractors (who were on mega bucks) out of bed to fix it. They would turn up to the office, spend 15 minutes there and leave again. To this day I still have no idea what they actually did but proportional to the amount of work done I think it had to be one of the best paid jobs in the world. That was what I was told my job would be, I could count the amount of times I had to call one of those guys out during the next 10 weeks on one hand. The job I ended up doing was very different.

After a few days doing this job (spending most of my time browsing Facebook and spending my wages on eBay) I was given a secondary job, this job ended up being the start of the rest of my life (I know that sounds super corny but it's true). This secondary job was to monitor all UK casualty reports, gather together information on what happened and put it together into a more comprehensive report. This is how it looked. Something would happen, like a contact, IED blast or an injury, the first report would come in on an instant messenger program, like a military version of MSN messenger (for those of you out there who remember it). It was pretty brief and would look something like this:

What is it?

When did it happen? - either exact time or roughly how long ago

Where did it happen? – A grid reference

What happened?

What's happening now?

What are you doing about it?

So, an example contact report might look like this

Contact
2 minutes ago
grid 123456
3 x enemy combatant
Sporadic 7.62 fire (basically means they're taking pot
shots with AK47 type rifles)
3 x Enemy KIA
1 x UK gunshot wound to leg (R)
Giving first aid

What follows next depends on what happened, if it was a
contact report where none of our guys got hurt that
would probably be it. However, if one of our guys got
hurt (like in the example above) then they would need to
be evacuated back to camp. This would be done in
what's called a '9 liner' and was used to give the Medical
Emergency Response Team (known as MERT) the
information they need to get the right kit ready, get to
the location and know what to expect when they get
there. MERT would usually consist of a doctor, a nurse,
a couple of paramedics and a bunch of RAF Regiment
gunners who would provide cover for the medics and
the casualty. Now let me be absolute clear on this. The
RAF get a lot of shit thrown at them (and a lot of it is
deserved) but the MERT team are fucking incredible and
as far as I'm concerned they represent the best of our
military, they will fly in to enemy fire in their Chinook,
grab the casualty, get them in the air and will give
treatment while flying, they can and have carried out
open heart surgery while in the air!

The 9 liner looks like this:

1. Location of pickup site
2. Frequency and call sign – Radio stuff so they can communicate on the way there
3. Patients by precedence – This is what kind of treatment they are likely to require. I.e. surgical, non-surgical, routine treatment etc
4. Special equipment – Specialist kit needed to get the casualty out, i.e. a winch, ventilation etc
5. Patients by type – can they walk on their own?
6. Security of pickup area – Are there bad guys near, are they firing on you?
7. Method of Marking – Using flares, flashing beacons, or other ways to show where you are
8. Patient Nationality
9. NBC contamination – Is there a Nuclear, Biological or Chemical threat?

After this would come another report specifically about the casualty so the MERT team knew what kind of treatment they would be giving, this is known as a MIST report:

M – Mechanism of injury – gunshot wound, RPG, IED etc

I – Type of Injury

S – Signs – Vital signs of patient

T – Treatment Given

Well this is a fucking laugh riot isn't it? Let's take a break and have a laugh at my expense.

A few years before any of this I worked as a barman in a shit hole of a pub back up North. I got to know the regulars in this place pretty well, one better than anyone else. She was a young lass, she was in her early 20's, slim build, good figure, light brown hair very cheerful but she was seriously aesthetically challenged. I mean she really did have a face for radio. Well Doris (As she will be known here) took a liking to me and regularly reminded me of this, she would send me messages asking if I wanted to pop around hers for a quickie (sorry mum). I politely turned down her offers until one day I had a moment of weakness. I was a horny 20-year-old, bored at home and got a text asking if I fancied a shag. We've all been there, standards go out the window and every hole becomes viable a goal, so I thought 'Fuck it' and went to pay her a visit.

I got to the house and instantly realised my mistake. It was a total bomb site, there was cigarette ends everywhere you looked, it stank of smoke, a little terrier dog was lying in the lounge looking like it was waiting to die, half an X-box on the stairs with the other half scattered across the hallway floor. This place did nothing to get me in the mood, but I was already there, I couldn't just walk out. I figured I might as well just get this out the way, so we went upstairs to her bedroom and got going. A few minutes in I realised this was going to be a challenge, while frantically pumping away I made the mistake of looking at her face, instantly little Pete decided to go on strike. Not only was this going to be a challenge, it just wasn't going to happen at all. I needed to get out of there. I continued giving it my best effort with what was effectively like pushing a marshmallow into a letter box. I figured the only way out was to fake it and leave, so that's what I did. I made all the right noises, got up, threw the rubber in the bin and walked out without another word. Walking past the shattered Xbox, the dog who had given up hope and through the smog, I was still fastening my belt as I walked out of the front door.

I thought that would be it, apart from a few awkward looks in the pub she would never want to speak to me again (I was fine with this by the way). But no, an hour later I got a message saying that was amazing and we should do it again (What the fuck?). Not only that but she told all her mates in the pub about it and how we were now seeing each other. I politely turned down any future advances but had to have an awkward conversation with her friends about why I wasn't interested anymore. Oh, by the way, the best man at my wedding with Kel told this story in the form of a poem, in front of my family and friends. Thanks Simo, wanker.

Right, now that I've firmly embarrassed myself, back to the grind. So, we've got an initial contact report, a 9 liner and the MIST report. I'd take this information and add it to a Microsoft PowerPoint presentation, describe what happened, place on a map where it happened, and add an update about what's happened since. Sometimes that would be it. Other times they'd retrieve some form of video of the incident, helmet cam footage, apache gun tape (The Apache choppers have powerful cameras on board) or footage from an unmanned aircraft (UAV). These videos would be put into a folder on the computer network. I'd find it, watch it to make sure it was useable and make sure it was the correct incident. I'd then include a link to that video in the report I'd created and that was it. Each night I'd send off this report to some unknown Lieutenant Colonel to do whatever he'd do with it. That's the whole process. I would get reports of death and injury, sometimes I would watch it on video and then send it off to the powers that be, I did this role for 10 weeks on nights, **on my own.**

Now for some civvys out there you might be reading this and thinking 'What's the big deal? I've seen loads of snuff videos on the net. Well firstly, fuck you. Secondly this isn't some random person on the internet, these are real lads and lasses with real families back home. They are in the same shit hole as us with the same mission objective as us. Trust me when I say it becomes very real and very raw over there, it's not just a news report or some 'gross' video on the internet while you're sitting in your pants eating chocolate in front of a monitor.

Chapter 9

Well this is shit

I must not tell new recruits that I killed a man with his own toe nail

We're at the point in the book where things start going south and there's a couple of things to be aware of here. Firstly, some of the stuff I talk about in here might bring stuff up for folks who have served in a war zone or experienced trauma in their lives. I said at the start of this book that I would keep it true to life and as brutally honest as possible and I still intend on doing that. What I would say to you guys is take care of yourself, if you notice it affecting you then take a break and there's no shame in skipping this chapter. Secondly an associated symptom of PTSD is repressed memories, with therapy and time I've managed to drag up a few of these memories and dealt with them properly but I'm sure there is some still hiding away in there somewhere. It has also screwed the timeline in my head so from this point on in the book the timeline of events may be a little all over the place, I'll do my best to keep it in some kind of order.

'Come on then Pete tell us what happened!' Alright, calm down imaginary person. Well, I spent the next 10 weeks watching people get seriously hurt and killed; usually in horrifically violent ways. Here's the thing about death, often it's not a peaceful or clean thing, even when people die of natural causes, it's usually pretty grim. And in a war zone this is especially true, when someone is killed at war it's probably going to be violent and destressing for everyone involved, most people aren't accustomed to witnessing this kind of stuff (and so they shouldn't be). At first, I didn't find it too bad, particularly as when we first got there it was poppy harvest season, so the insurgents and Taliban were busy farming. Also, the videos hadn't started then. I'd get a report, log it and go back to doing what I was doing (usually not a lot). We had a few contact reports where the bad guys fired a few rounds and ran off or maybe one of them would catch a round. As the poppy harvest ended, things started to get worse. One incident saw a lad be incredibly unlucky and take a round through the side of his body armour, the one area that didn't have ballistic plates in, I think that was the first time I sat back in my seat and thought 'fuck'. It began to feel real, raw, these weren't just names on a monitor or spoken by a news presenter, these were real people, lads like me, just in a different branch of the same military and I'd just watched their life end in a fucking horrendous way and in a level of gruesome detail that most people aren't accustomed to.

On another occasion a convoy was hit by an IED blast. I think one was killed in that and 3 others seriously injured, they sent through some pictures of that and the vehicle looked like it was never a vehicle, twisted and crumpled metal, contorted beyond all recognition. I still don't know how anyone made it out of that. I can remember fairly early doors into this role a lad manning a gun mounted on a Jackal took a round to the head, killed him instantly. Shit like this seemed to happen on a daily basis. But this is the reality of a war zone, awful things happen to good people, lives get changed in an instant, and not just for the person hit but for their families, friends, the lads who were with them, the medics who treated them. I've heard civvys saying things like 'The media hides what really happens over there'. Of course they fucking do! If you were told everything that went on over there, you'd be getting berated by constant reports of death and injury, and in heart wrenching detail, you'd hear about children stepping on landmines and being scattered across the sand, you'd hear about insurgents strapping explosives to a donkey and sending it in to a check point manned by our lads. It's for your own good that you don't get told all of this because trust me, it takes its toll. The media give you a stripped down, clean version of what goes on, the bare minimum detail and this is exactly how it should be.

Unfortunately, this means that you don't often hear about the good that went on over there. The schools, clinics and houses that were built over there by coalition forces. Girls feeling safe to get an education and people made to feel safe to set up a market stall and make some money for their family. Additionally, the hundreds of locals given jobs by the forces, able to make an honest living and keep out of trouble. Thing is, now that we've left a lot of this has gone back to shit again. The Taliban knew we were leaving so they waited till we did just that and strolled back in again and re-fucked everything up again.

A few times some of our guys were killed by insurgents who had infiltrated the Afghan Army or police, they'd wait for the right time and then kill as many of our guys as they could before been taken down. Almost every day a new report came through, another lad killed or maimed, it became the norm and after a while. It got fucking exhausting and every time it happened it pissed me off more and more. I sat there desperately wanting to help, I'd pace up and down the office, go outside and try to think of what I could do to help, but there was nothing I could do. For a start, I'm a comms techy in the RAF, I wouldn't have lasted 10 minutes out there. I had no way of getting out there, didn't know where I was going or have any decent kit, I'd never seen combat. I was kidding myself trying to work out how I could help but I couldn't shake this sense of helplessness. I stayed put and cracked on with my job while feeling completely useless, like a bystander just watching good lads being killed in really shitty ways,

Maybe I should have but I didn't realise at the time that it was starting to take its toll. I began to hate the Afghans, not just in the general sense but a raw, thorough hatred of them, all of them, even the innocent ones. The anger and the feeling of uselessness chewed away at me. I started binge eating food from parcels sent in by friends, family and charities then making myself throw up in the toilet, this happened 4 or 5 times. I don't know why I did this, I just felt the compulsion to do it, but at the time, in a weird way, it made sense. I started doing other weird shit as well, I found two little sumo wrestler figures, they were covered in sticky stuff, the idea was you would mush them together throw them on a table and it would look like they were wrestling. I spent 4 hours one night putting them in every sexual position I could think of and taking photos while pissing myself laughing. I made an album on my laptop and called it 'sumosutra'. I would patrol the office with a fly swatter or my beret while narrating out-loud the adventures of 'the fly sniper', looking back this is pretty funny but a bit mental as well. It's amazing what your brain thinks up when you're bored but even now, I can't help shake the feeling that I should have spotted then that something was going wrong and I should have spoken to someone. That's the thing with the forces mentality, the 'crack on' attitude is great for when something needs to get done urgently but we tend to take it into every aspect of our lives where it can do more harm than good.

I can still remember the incident that affected me the worst there. A young marine took a round to the neck, MERT got to him and evacuated him to Bastion, he survived the whole way with the medics on board grafting away in stupid heat, pressure, noise and dirty conditions, doing everything in their power to keep him alive. He survived until they landed, then he passed away as they touched down. Except this wasn't one incident. While I was writing this chapter, I pulled up a list on the internet of UK deaths in Afghan during June-August 2011 (something which I've always been tempted to do but avoided until now) so I could try and keep it to a timeline. I learnt something interesting. This was two incidents that my brain somehow combined into one. The marine was injured by a grenade whilst on patrol, he was the one who got back to Bastion and then died, it was another lad (I think from 1 rifles) who took a round to the neck. I can't remember what happened to him though, since I can't find any details about the incident hopefully that means he lived.

I still remember most of what happened with that marine. I got the 9 liner and MIST through. I don't know what it was, but something about it took me back, a while later an update came through that he had died of his wounds. It hit me like a tonne of shit, I slumped back in my seat, finding it difficult to process. I think it was around 12am and the mess (food hall) for late workers was open so I decided to get myself away for a bit and left for some food. As I left the building I looked to my right and saw the MERT Chinook on 'Nightingale'. This was the emergency chopper landing pad. There was a body being stretchered off the back ramp covered in a sheet. I don't know if it was the same guy or not but, in my mind, it was. That one stuck with me for years and even now, 7 years later, this has been seriously tough to write.

I always felt like a dick because this stuff affected me in this way, I've never been in combat, I've never had a bullet fly past my head, I never saw any of these guys get hit in person. I didn't know any of them, so why did it bother me so much? For years I felt guilty. If I spoke to someone who has experienced that type of stuff, it's like I'm not worthy of feeling like this compared to them, I felt like a fraud, as if I was somehow trying to get attention or sympathy even though I didn't tell anyone about this stuff for a long time. I guess the mind can only take so much exposure to death and violence before the stress becomes too much. Eventually I had to learn that sometimes you've got no control in what your mind does, it'll react however it chooses to react and it's nothing to do with how tough you are or how anyone else dealt with anything else. You're not them, you're you.

When one of our guys was killed in theatre there was a strict protocol to follow. As soon as the person was declared dead an order would be sent around all UK personnel in Afghan to cease non-operational comms to anywhere outside of Afghan. The internet on each base would be turned off, welfare phone lines would be blocked, only certain people could communicate with the outside world and it had to be essential operational stuff. The idea is that it would allow their next of kin to be notified through the proper channels rather than finding out from Facebook or a phone call. I heard it came about when a lad was killed in Iraq, his family ended up finding out through family calling and messaging their condolences. The whole thing was known as 'Op Minimise' (as in to minimise comms). A loudspeaker announcement would go out across the base letting everyone know. I used to find this really tough, especially when it was one of the guys who I'd received reporting or a video of. All I could think about was their family were about to be told their loved one wasn't coming home alive or someone was going to have to learn to live life minus a major part of their body and I found it fucking heart wrenching every time. Because I slept during the day, I'd often be woken up by an Op Minimise announcement, I'd could feel the anger and sadness building every time, it became really raw for me. I felt fucking stupid because it was never an issue for anybody else but my role seemed to give me a unique insight each case and an in-depth awareness of what was really going on out there.

A couple of days after a death all the UK personnel who could make it would get together for a vigil service. It was a religious and military ceremony for everyone to pay their respects. I'm not a religious man at all but I always found these pretty poignant. I think everyone did, so I'd always make a point of getting up early, well before my shift started so I could attend. All UK bases across Afghan would try to have their own service at the same time (when the insurgent fuck wits weren't having a pop). The Bastion vigil was thousands of people who would form up in a horseshoe around the memorial with the padre (priest) along with a few guys from the unit the person belonged to. I remember on one occasion I was stood about 7 ranks back, everyone looking smart and completely silent while the padre spoke. I noticed 2 lads a few ranks ahead of me not stood in rank, they were hugging each other and both of them crying, it was obvious they knew the lad who had been killed, this crushed all of us. Most of us didn't know the lad who had been killed so you usually manage to maintain this emotional distance but with 2 of his mates stood right there not able to hold back the pain it was fucking brutal. Despite being powerful for me, I secretly hated these vigil services. It was important to me to pay my respects, so I always went when I could but for me it felt like the perfect storm of shittyness. I was one of the first notified of the contact and their death. I heard (or sometimes saw) the body land at nightingale and a day or so later I would see footage or pictures of what happened. It was a reminder that their family was about to find out that they would never see their loved one alive again.

Although I found a lot of what I saw tough going I never thought it could create any kind of lasting issue. I didn't even see making myself throw up as a problem. Looking back on that stuff I don't know the psychological reason why, but I see it as my mind was trying to protect me from what was going on. The brain is a really fucked up thing, it can make you do things and you don't know why, it can make you do other shit and you don't even realize you're doing it. Stuff you would expect to mess you up doesn't and the stuff you expect to just brush off like watching a news report screws with your mind.

Chapter 10

Out of the frying pan and into the fire

SAC White must not leopard crawl around the office

I did warn you some parts of this book would be grim, well strap in, there's more to come.

After 10 weeks I was replaced by one of the lads I arrived in Bastion with. I don't know why but my guess is, the sergeant who was in the bed space next to me spotted something wasn't right when I got back every morning, plus I was fucking knackered, 10 weeks of 13-hour night shifts with no days off will do that to you. Me and this lad swapped jobs, he took my job and I took his job working on the service desk. I was kind of gutted about this at first, I felt like I had a cushy thing going at the old job (apart from, you know, all the death).

While I was in Kandahar the entire squadron started a charity fitness challenge where we would use gym kit to run, walk, row or cycle the distance between Kandahar and RAF Leeming (around 7,300 Km). I jumped right into this and ended up smashing off a load of miles to contribute towards the effort. When I found out about getting shipped over to Bastion, I told the guys I'd carry it on and send my distance completed over to them weekly. It was important for me, not only because some of my family and mates had donated towards the fundraising, but I wanted to remain part of the squadron effort. Not wanting to be a jack bastard I kept my word and grafted hard, sweating my tits off in the heat so I could help out. 3 weeks into my time in Bastion and sending over my distance each week I'd heard nothing back, so I called the corporal I had been working under in Kandahar, he told me that they hadn't been counting my distance as part of it and he didn't know why I was bothering. This may sound petty, but this royally pissed me off. I had offered to help out the team and they'd just completely ignored me. But spite is one of the greatest motivators, so I thought 'fuck them, I'll do it myself'. I set out to complete the whole distance myself which meant doing 81km every day while I was there. Honestly, I don't remember how close I got, I know I didn't finish it because I ended up lifting a lot of weights but I know I took a good chunk out of it, probably about 5000 Km. This nicely sums up the mentality of a lot of the folks in the RAF, there's none of this 'brotherhood' or looking out for each other bullshit. Folks will fuck each other over in a heartbeat, and sometimes not even to get ahead, sometimes just because they feel like being a cock.

I started working on the service desk in late July 2011, basically we were the whipping boy for anyone who had issues with IT. Usually password resets and other menial bullshit. The perverse thing was this was the first time I had a job that would have an immediate impact on things going on in Afghan, making sure other people with more important jobs could actually do those jobs. Did it feel like I was making a difference though? Fuck no. I was basically the lowest of the low IT techs, 3 of us covered all the basic IT stuff for thousands of folks, and we grafted hard, shifts were 12 hours long and most days you worked every minute of those 12 hours only stopping for a fag break. I had never smoked before I went to Afghan and I've never smoked since getting back but smoking over there meant getting some precious minutes rest.

It didn't help that the 2 army lads I worked with would fail an IQ test even if they cheated and were about as much use as tits on a fish. Even though I was grafting like a bastard it felt like a relief to get away from the shitty stuff that had been going on, my mind was busy and I wasn't forced to witness death and injury every shift. At least that's how it seemed at first. Part of the new job was something called 'impexing'; it was a seriously dull process which involved moving data between different classified systems. For example, moving a file/picture or video from a restricted system to a secret system in a way that didn't risk any data security (see, I told you it was dull). On the face of it there's nothing wrong with this task but given that we were in a war zone where shitty stuff happened all the time, some of the stuff we had to move across was inevitably going to be shitty, and let's not kid ourselves here, some of it was really interesting. Sometimes we'd get detailed interrogation reports of senior Taliban figures. These things were ace. Now sorry to disappoint you but I didn't see any reports of bamboo under finger nails, waterboarding or Russian roulette. As much as I wanted to see that shit it just didn't seem to go on. What actually went on were the ultimate mind games by the world champions of fucking with your head. The guys who do these interrogations are full on psychological ninjas. Imagine having an argument with your missus and she's talking circles around you, well take the emotion out of that and up the ante by a thousand. I used to love seeing these reports. Not that I ever read them for entertainment with a huge smile in my face seeing the process of breaking these guys down, it always to check the integrity of the data of course...

We also got a fair amount of shitty stuff, photos, videos etc of incidents, I never knew what they were for, but my thinking is they were part of investigations into what happened. There was nothing special about these, you can see a lot of the same stuff on the internet if that kind of thing takes your fancy. Like I mentioned before though, everything becomes rawer over there and after the shit I had just worked with in the previous 10 weeks, seeing this stuff bothered me. This time it was different, although we did have a few bits coming through of our guys getting hurt most of it was recordings and pictures of bad guys getting hit, things like apache gun tapes of hellfire missiles or .30 cal making them go pop, UAV videos of them getting killed. Some of them were pictures of the dead bad guys and their belongings. Now this was a different ball game. I FUCKING LOVED THIS SHIT.

Right, now you may be reading this and thinking 'You sick bastard, those are human beings'. Well, firstly, if that's what you're thinking the rest of this book is going to be an uncomfortable read for you. Secondly, I'd just spent 10 weeks watching these same bad guys injure and kill our guys, I felt like I was finally watching us get some pay back on these wankers, can you really blame me? All that frustration of me not being able to do a fucking thing about what was going on could be released when I looked at this stuff. I didn't just enjoy it, it became like watching sport. On night shifts when the other guys were sat watching movies on their laptops I was 'impexing' and watching these movies and pictures of insurgents being killed on repeat, loving every second of it. Now I'm not going to pretend this isn't fucked up, of course it is and looking back, it should have been a clear sign that something was going wrong inside my noggin, but this was my way of coping with what I'd witnessed and to me it seemed like a reasonable thing to do.

After a while this became a bit of an addiction, because the two other guys I worked with were useless I kind of became the unofficial leader of the service desk so when I delegated the jobs, I made sure I would get all the impexing jobs and I made sure to do a REALLY thorough job. Eventually this would bite me in the arse. Like a smack head, eventually they were going to get a bad batch of smack. One night while working through the impexing jobs I found a PowerPoint presentation that needed transferring across. It was a presentation that the intel guys in the UK forces would show low level insurgents, usually poor farmers who the Taliban would offer some money to so they would plant IED or lob a grenade over a compound wall. The presentation was full of fucking horrible images of the consequences of their actions and what the Taliban got up to. I don't remember a lot of what was in this presentation, my

60

brain has tucked most of it away in a dark corner somewhere, but the one image that was stuck in there was one of a child, probably about 3 years old, his body was completely burnt, he was lying on the side of the road, it looked like he had been shot first, then set on fire. I don't know who his child was, I had no connection to him. At the time of writing this chapter I don't have any kids of my own (as far as I know anyway) but this hit me like a fucking train. I left the tent and had a fag. I've never told anyone this part before, even when discussing this picture in therapy, but after seeing this, I sat down somewhere quiet beside a shipping container and cried. I think I must have had 4 fags before I felt like I could go back to work. I don't remember much of that shift but as far as I know I just carried on and finished the job whilst my head was in turmoil, acting like everything was fine.

It was at this time that I started doing guard like the rest of the lads had to, because I had been on night shifts and I was the only person doing that job I'd manage to avoid it but now I was as eligible as the next man. Guard shifts were 24 hours long, they'd come around every couple of weeks, you'd team up with 2 others from any unit in the base and get assigned a sanger (concrete guard tower). The sangers had 3 floors, the bottom floor had a camp cot and fridge stocked full of bottles of water. The second floor had another camp cot and we'd store all our kit there. The top floor was the observation level, it had a 360° view. There was a table with a radio and a shit load of ammunition on it and if you got lucky (because they were in seriously short supply) a night vision monocular. I won't discuss the shifts in detail, but everyone would each take turns on guard while one or 2 others got their head down in the most uncomfortable beds on the planet. Not only was it hot as hell, you had to sleep in your kit in case anything kicked off. On my first ever guard stint I opened my eyes to see a camel spider 2 metres away from me. If you've never heard of a camel spider then google it, they're actually pretty harmless but fucking terrifying things to see. I didn't sleep a wink for the rest of that shift, that's the most exciting thing that happened that entire 24 hour shift, apart from making some ration pack bombs which consists of emptying the heating crystals from a ration pack into a plastic bottle, pour in some water, put the cap back on, shake, throw and enjoy the resulting bang and the guard commander shouting down the radio "Whoever is throwing those rat pack bombs knock it off!".

My second guard was much more eventful. Opposite this particular sanger there were 3 local compounds about 700 yards away. At about 3am in the morning I was on guard while the other 2 lads were in the levels below. While looking through the night vision sight to pass the time I spotted a local leaving the largest compound and start walking directly towards my tower. Considering there was nothing between the tower and him except a field and a massive fence I thought it was a bit odd, so I kept an eye on him. He just kept coming, I fired a pen flare into the air (a pen launcher that fires mini flares) so he knew we were watching him. Nothing, he didn't even look at the tower or the flare, he just kept walking. I called one of the lads up from the level below, he took a look and decided to give the guard commander a heads up in case things got emotional and we needed the Quick Reaction Force (QRF) to do the actual soldiering. In the mean time I decided to fire a flare in the guys general direction as a 'What the fuck are you doing!?' kind of thing. Still nothing. With my arsehole twitching like a rabbit's nose, I shouldered my rifle and along with the lad next to me (a really young Army driver) we discussed what to do next. He got back on the radio ready to ask for some help while I watched this bloke through my scope. I was thinking "Holy shit, I'm a 21 year RAF geek and I'm about to shoot this bastard'. He was about 200 yards away now and I was getting ready to cock my rifle, trying to remember our rules of engagement to work out if I need to fire a warning shot or just shoot him. Right at that moment he stops, drops his trousers and begins to take a shit in the field, still paying no attention to us. I nearly shot a guy for taking a shit. He knew exactly what he was doing though, he could have walked in any direction to get some privacy, so why did he walk 200 yards towards the Afghans biggest main operating base? To show us what he thought of us, wanker.

Later that morning, about 7 am I was getting my head down on the bottom level when the lads on top called me up, I got up just in time to see a fecking huge explosion about a mile out, throwing up a huge plume of sand and dust. Turns out an American patrol had got some local intel about an IED on the side of a road and did a control detonation on it, apparently this wasn't even a particularly big one but the power these things throw out is mega. At the time I found it pretty interesting but later on I found myself thinking about the lads who got hit by these things, it made sense why people got killed by them, even in armoured vehicles.

I did the service desk job for about 4 weeks before my tour was coming to an end, by this point the Staff Sergeant who ran the IT section had taken a liking to me (not in that way, you weirdo) and a disliking to the other two lads that I worked with so he told me to take more time off during each day and leave them to it. His idea was that because I would be leaving, and they still had another 2 months left on their tour they were going have to learn to take care of themselves without me there to baby sit them. Each day I took some time out to get to the gym (I'd become a bit of a machine by this point because of the amount of gym time I'd done), spent some time on the welfare computers catching up with the outside world, sometimes I just took a walk-through camp listening to music and spent some time sunbathing. This felt like the first time I had relaxed for the entire tour. One day I had a chat with the lad who I had swapped jobs with earlier in the tour. I was keen to ask him what his experience of it was. I don't remember what he said word for word, but his experience was pretty similar to mine. They had stopped including the videos but kept up the reporting and pictures. Then he told me something which pissed me right off. The whole job was bullshit. It never existed before we got there and when we had finished it ceased to exist again. The night watchman job was just created because we were surplus man power and they didn't know where else to put me. The day watchman job was legit, and he had loads of work on but didn't do any of the casualty reporting stuff. So basically, I'd just spent 10 weeks of my life getting mentally fucked up for nothing. As far as I'm aware, those emails, I sent off with the reports in weren't even needed. If I had any faith in my chain of command, it was gone. Because the job didn't officially exist that's why I was working on my own; I had no superior in charge of me and there was no real work to do. Not only had I done this job which would later be the foundation for my mental health crisis, but I felt like I'd wasted almost my entire time on tour achieving nothing. First spending a month doing jack shit at Kandahar, then 10 weeks doing a non-existent job at Bastion. The only part of my time there that meant anything was on the service desk and even that was limited in terms of the impact it allowed me to make. I felt seriously let down by my CoC, during my entire time in JFCIS nobody ever checked that I was OK, I didn't have any kind of manager or even anyone to talk to, but to top it all off there was never any need for me to go through any of that in the first place.

My last week on tour was ace, our replacements had got there and had taken over. Now we were playing the waiting game; waiting to return home. Loads of sunbathing, catching up on sleep and lots of gym time. I was a bit of a fatty when I got to Afghan and generally unfit. By the time I left I'd lost 3 stone and was in the best shape of my life. I'm sure the insane heat helped in this and I guess making myself throw up had a hand in it but it's a fucking miserable and stupid way to lose weight, that's not why I did it. I still don't know why I did that. It's what I've now come to know as the Afghan diet, spend nearly 5 months working long shifts in blistering heat, work out at least an hour a day and gorge on sweets before sticking your fingers down your throat.

Chapter 11

I'm fine, I promise

SAC White must not use a loose server rack door as a riot shield while throwing pens at my corporal

Our flight out of Bastion was delayed 24 hours due to some technical issue on the plane, we all made the most of it, getting some gym time in, sunbathing and sleeping but everyone was fucking knackered and we all just wanted to get home. Finally, we got away, 15 minutes into the flight out of Afghan pretty much every single person on that plane was asleep except me. Sat in my chair, feeling the relief of going home I tried to take stock of my tour. I was excited to go to Afghanistan to be a part of the war effort, I wanted to contribute and make a difference, even if it was small, But I couldn't shake the feeling that the whole thing had been a waste. I'd done a lot of growing up in the last four and a half months and saw a part of the world and a side of life that not many do. I was thankful for this, but I still felt like I'd failed in my objective of making a difference.

I saw one of the air hostess types making their way down the aisle with one of their trolleys, that's when I clocked that they were handing out cans of cold beer. After 5 months of no booze in a desert that was hotter than Satan's arse hole this was the best tasting beer I've ever had. We flew into Cyprus for decompression. After a few months in a war zone you're generally pretty pent up, pretty tired and feeling absorbed by the reality of war. The idea of decompression is to unwind, get some rest and try to process what's been going on. What it actually is, is 24 hours getting pissed, catching up on some sleep and having enforced fun; this fun consisted of movies, swimming, water skiing and some kind of stage show, usually stand-up comedy or a band. the theory is after doing all this, you're better placed to get back to normal life with less risk of issues.

Let's just get this clear, after 4-7 months in a war zone where some folks have seen others get killed or in some cases have killed others, constantly sleep deprived, grafting their arse off, working long shifts and at some level constantly on edge, 24 hours getting pissed and swimming will make all of this OK? Get fucked! Don't get me wrong, it's nice to have a mini holiday to unwind a bit but there's no chance lads and lasses are going to feel psychologically prepared to get back to civilian life in 24 hours after all that shit. I expected to have a sit-down chat with at least one person trained to see early signs of psych issues in people but that didn't happen. I still didn't know that anything was wrong with me but there's a good chance that a chat with someone trained to spot the signs might have raised the alarm bells early.

Anyway, personally I spent my time getting drunk (on 3 cans of cheap lager), falling asleep in the cinema. I tried my hand at water skiing (which I was useless at) and more sleeping. We were delayed a further 24 hours here because of more aircraft issues. It wouldn't have been so bad if you weren't expecting to see your family only to be told you need to wait longer. For me this whole period is one big drunken daze which consisted largely of strictly controlled, enforced fun. One flight and a massive bus journey later we got back to RAF Leeming, we drove into our equipment hangar where a bunch of our families were waiting. My folks and Kel were all there. As soon as I got off the bus Kel ran at me and nearly knocked me over, she never has been the shy and retiring type.

Getting home was ace, I felt relaxed for the first time in months, I could get a decent shower, catch up on sleep and release some of that *ahem* pent up frustration that 5 months deprived of sex leaves you with. Being a qualified therapist Kel was constantly checking I was OK. At the time I didn't know this, but she felt like something was different about me. I didn't want to be one of these 'thousand-yard stare' types who never spoke about their experiences, so I was relatively open about my tour. As far as I was concerned nothing special happened. I did hold some stuff back, particularly the details of some of the deaths and injuries I'd seen, purely because I didn't think anyone really wanted to know that shit. I mean how often does someone say 'I saw a burnt dead child the other day'. It's not really a conversation starter is it? The clues were there though, I just didn't know what I was looking for.

About 2 months after getting back I had my first little 'episode'. We were watching a documentary about the TA (Territorial Army) and the work they do in Afghan. I was keen for Kel to watch it with me because it would save me time explaining what it's like there, aside from 'a big, hot, windy, sandy, shit hole'. A big chunk of the program was talking about medical roles, it was focusing on a doctor in civvy street and in the TA, showing the work they do. This doc was working out of Bastion, it showed them getting an injured Brit soldier from nightingale and into the hospital. After that I don't remember anything. I know I was watching the TV, but I'd completely zoned out. I knew where I was and what was on the TV but that was about it. It was like I was sleeping but with my eyes open. Kel had been trying to get my attention for a few minutes until she finally grabbed my arm and I snapped out of it. I had no fucking idea what had just happened, the lights were on, but nobody was home. Looking back, I don't think it was a flashback because I wasn't reliving anything or seeing any visions, maybe it was? I don't know. It was like although I knew where I was and what was going on around me, on an emotional level, I was going through it again and my brain and I didn't know how to deal with it so I just turned into some sort of zombie watching this programme. What the fuck was that?

This happened again a couple of weeks later I was sat in the pub with Kel and a bunch of mates, we were drinking and having a good time. I was telling one of the guys some funny shit from my tour. When I finished my story and his attention naturally shifted elsewhere, I looked out of the window for a second and again I spaced out. I knew I was looking out the window and people were around me, but I didn't move, speak or look anywhere else but out the window, just staring into nothingness. It took a mate of mine grabbing me to get my attention again.

Before we left for our tour the medical guys told us that it could take us a few weeks after we got back to adjust, and we might have some weird shit going on. They also said this was normal and don't stress over it. So, I didn't. I just forgot about it and cracked on as normal. This is pretty common in forces circles, ignoring stuff with our health that really shouldn't be ignored. There's a major 'man up and crack on' mentality which sometimes is great. When the shit is really hitting the fan and you need people to react quickly and correctly to what's going on this works great because a second's delay can cost lives. However, it tends to bleed into other aspects of life as well because people don't know where to draw the line and there's a fear that you'll be seen as weak if you say anything. I'll probably mention this a few times in this book but the 'man up' mentality is bullshit and has contributed to so many suicides of servicemen and women that it should be considered some kind of poison in its own right. If you're going through a shit time, manning up isn't putting your head in the sand and keeping quiet, manning up is having the balls to say 'hey I'm a bit fucked here and I need some help' and the sooner this mentality gets adopted by the forces in general the more lives will be saved and the less people will have to go through a shit time.

The next few weeks of my leave passed without any further weirdness (at least as far that I'm aware of). My leave finished and I went back to work, back to the usual office bullshit, trying (and failing) to find some decent work and taking prolonged shit breaks so I could play Angry Birds. Every now and then I'd get one of my civvy mates telling me that I seemed 'different' with some of them saying I was distant and like my mind wasn't in the room. I never felt like that except for the two times I mentioned above. Looking back now I think I was gradually showing some signs of depression and PTSD but as usual I didn't notice or pay attention to it. How do you even know you're suffering depression without anyone telling you what you're looking for or having experienced it? I always thought it was just feeling sad (it's really not). Because I thought I was fine I just kept telling people I was fine. I wasn't, I just didn't know it yet.

Chapter 12

I'm not fine

I must not suggest to my station commander that he attend equality training to show him why he's equal to me. He's not, he's better than me.

I was itching for another deployment, I wanted an opportunity to feel useful, especially since my first one had been wasted on bullshit jobs. I really wanted to get out into the shit, not doing some cushy bullshit like I had before but doing a job that made a difference and ideally, where I was able to take out some bad guys. I knew this was a bullshit wish because we don't do that shit in my line of work but the anger that started to bubble up in me in Afghan was still simmering away and I wanted to get even. I wanted an excuse to get violent. In July 2012, I got my wish of another tour but not in the way that I expected. A private security contracting company (who I won't name but we all know who they are) managed to fuck up their contract for providing security at the London Olympics by failing to provide several thousand guards and fail to equip and train loads more. This meant that the military had to put up around 24,000 bods to fill the gap, I was one of them.

I was one of the fortunate ones, I hadn't been deployed for nearly a year and I was given a few weeks' notice. Some of the other guys had only been back from a deployment to Afghan or Iraq for a couple of weeks when they were told (imagine telling your wife and kids that you were leaving again after only being back for 2 weeks, talk about being shit on). We didn't know much about what we would be doing but the idea of helping out at the Olympics was a once in a lifetime opportunity.

During the last few months I'd started to feel miserable, I was constantly tired, I wasn't enjoying things that I used to, in fact I wasn't really feeling any emotions much anymore. I was feeling empty as a person. The whole lack of emotions thing is difficult to explain, imagine holding the new born baby of your best mate and feeling absolutely nothing (this happened to me by the way). The space in your mind that would normally be filled with emotion is just filled with emptiness. I couldn't feel happiness, surprise, joy, excitement, basically any kind of positive emotion. The only emotion I could recognise was anger, which if you're going to only feel one emotion, that's a pretty shite one to be left with. Before we started prep for the Olympics role, I told Kel that I wasn't feeling right, and she told me to speak to the Doc. But I didn't want to admit to anyone in an official capacity that I wasn't right, I only went to the doc if I had no choice in the matter. I didn't want to risk not going to the Olympics or fucking up my career, so I didn't make an appointment.

After a week-long security training course in what was essentially the exact same set up as the airport security lanes (which was actually pretty interesting) we all left for the Olympics. We were spread across different sites where the games were being held. I was sent to the Olympic park which given the options was by far the best one to work at. It was massive, everything was brand new, looked brilliant and most Olympic events were held there. I won't explain the layout to you because you can find all you want about it on the interweb in much more detail than I could go into. The other positive was that our accommodation was decent. We were camped out in a field a few miles down the road. Half of us were in glorified shipping containers with bunk beds (known as 'the ghetto' or 'tin town'). The rest of us (including myself) lucked out and got the accommodation that the civvy security 'no shows' were meant to be in. These were pods normally used for festivals. The rooms were tiny, but they had 2 comfy as fuck beds in, storage, en-suite bathroom. For 2 lads to live in for a few weeks they were properly cramped but luxury compared to anything else the military had ever put us up in. The army sorted the food out which, to be fair, was mega. What those guys can do with some pots and glorified BBQs in a couple of tents puts civvy chefs to shame.

The actual job we were doing was decent, even if the days were seriously long.; We had 12 rows of 10 airport style security lanes where folks would come in, get their bags and bodies scanned, get searched if needs be then crack on. I worked on the VIP security lanes which was great. I couldn't really give a shit about celebrities but sometimes it was interesting seeing who was coming through. During the opening ceremony we had the cast of the expendables come through; then Yoko Ono, Cliff Richard, John Bishop, loads of Olympians. For me one of the more interesting parts of the job was the security they had going on. As well as loads of armed police knocking about; every now and then we'd get very average looking blokes through carrying a back pack that would walk straight through the checkpoint without being checked. These were either special forces or counter terrorist police. The back packs had stripped down rifles inside, snipers were dotted around roof tops and the 'sneaky beaky' guys were constantly gathering their intel, not that you would ever know it, I love that shit. I've always been interested in what goes on behind the scenes to keep people secure.

Because the rules for what people could bring in were the same as airplanes, we spent most of our time confiscating pointless shit from them. Bottles of perfume they'd just bought from the shopping centre next to us, a drinking glass someone packed for a picnic. We took a few Stanley knives and pocket knives off people, most were just people who genuinely forget they had them. I once had to take a really old pocket knife of an old fella, he told me he'd had it since he was 16, his dad gave it to him, and he'd carried it every day since. It killed me to take that off him, he clearly wouldn't harm anyone with it. When we confiscated things, we had to put it into a clear plastic bin, people would always ask us if they could come back and get it when they left but we'd always say no because shifts would usually change so nobody would be there to recognise them. In the case of this old fella, because I'm a soft bastard and I really felt for him, I said I would work late and be there for him to collect it. I waited for a few hours and had to leave to get some kip before my next shift but as far as

I'm aware he never came back. Chances are the knife got destroyed. When I was 18 my dad gave me a pen knife that I still use today, I still think what it would be like if I made it to this old fellas age and someone took that knife off me.

On a more positive note, I had one of my best moments in the military here. At the end of each day when people left the games, we'd stand by the massive exit gates to make sure no sneaky little bastards tried to get back in (loads of this stuff went on). I only got to do this duty once, but it was fucking brilliant. The way the public reacted to us was phenomenal, it was more in line with the way the yanks treat their military lads and lasses. We got our hands shook, photos, and hugs with everyone thanking us for helping out, this went on for a couple of hours while people were leaving. It was the first (and pretty much only) time I felt genuinely proud to serve, I was fucking buzzing!

My head gradually got more and more fucked during this time, not only was I feeling pretty fucking miserable, but I wasn't enjoying anything. I was still using my spare time to watch videos on the internet of insurgents getting killed because it gave me some entertainment. I realised that I was doing nothing in my down time (not that we had much of it), I wasn't sleeping much at night; getting to sleep was fine, but I was waking up at 2/3 am every night and couldn't get back to sleep. What was more worrying was I was a proper angry little bastard all the time. And not just being generally pissed off, I wanted to fight basically everyone, I'm really not an angry person. In fact, I'm a total pussy and I'll avoid conflict if I can but this all suddenly changed and everyone who did something wrong or might do something wrong one day deserved a slap. One day, a member of the public who was pissed up and kicking off inside the Olympic park, swearing at the Olympic volunteer (These guys were ace by the way, if you did this job then you are a legend!); a few people were trying to reason with him and calm him down, I just barged in, got in his face and told him *"Wind your fucking neck in or it's going to get emotional quickly"* while getting ready to nut him. Thankfully the police got there and escorted him out before I made an even bigger twat of myself. By some stroke of luck nothing ever came of that even though I really should have had my arse handed to me. When I wasn't threatening members of the public, I was finding people harder than me to pick a fight with. Usually paras. I don't really remember what happened with this one (Not because I got knocked out, because it's one of those things my brain has tucked away somewhere in my head), all I do know is that the lad I started picking a fight with knew that throttling some 23 year old RAF gobshite just wasn't worth the trouble. To go along with insane levels of anger were random periods of extreme sadness, I'd be walking and suddenly get an almost uncontrollable urge to cry, sometimes it was absolutely nothing that would set this off, sometimes it was randomly thinking things like "dogs die, yeah that's sad" and I'd be off, usually I fought off the urge to cry but it would just wash over me like a wave. It was completely mental!

It all got to a point where I couldn't ignore it anymore, it was obvious that something was going seriously wrong in the old noggin' and if I didn't do something about it now shit was going to go downhill rapidly. The next day I stood in the security lane at work doing the usual job while shitting myself that I was about to end my career and trying to work out what I was going to say and how I'd say it. I must have planned 50 different conversations and scenarios in my head, everything from them giving me a cuddle and telling me it was going to be OK to forcing happy pills down my neck and putting me in a padded room, I worked myself up so much that I decided I'd wait and see if things improved over the next day (because the last few months would somehow be all OK in the space of 24 hours).

The next day we had Boris Johnson come through the lane with his security team, these guys were like walking fridge freezers (the America style) and all of them were carrying weapons. None of the guys who were permitted to carry got searched (for obvious reasons) but as the first bodyguard walked through, the anger took over and I got an uncontrollable urge of 'who the fuck are you to walk straight through!?' and tried to stop him so I could search him and berate him for being an arrogant wanker. Now as to why I did this or what I hoped to get out of it, I have no idea. Thankfully he didn't walk straight through me like he could of, he stopped and politely showed me his ID which meant that he was carrying a firearm and didn't need to be searched. One of the guys I was working with (professionally) asked me what the fuck I was doing. I down played the whole thing and said that it was a lapse of concentration. That was my final clue (as if it were needed), that I needed to get this shit sorted.

First thing the next morning I went to the medical tent and asked to see the Doc. I was told before I saw the doc, I needed to speak to the nurse who would then decide if it needed the doc. A young army nurse sat down with me and asked what was going on, I explained to her how I'd been feeling miserable, I wasn't enjoying anything, I was constantly angry or uncontrollably sad, I couldn't sleep, and I was generally pretty fucked. No straight jacket yet, so far so good. She asked me if I knew where any of this came from, so I told her a very short version of what happened in Afghan. Half way through telling her she stopped me and said she was going to get the doctor, as she walked out the door she stopped, turned around and said, *"There's a lot of needles and sharp stuff in here, am I OK to leave you here with it?"* I told her it was fine but didn't realise this was the first of a shit load more times that I'd be asked if I was going to hurt myself. The doc came through (no straight jacket or happy pills in hand) and I explained all the same stuff again. She didn't tell me what she thought was going on but pretty quickly she told me that I was going to be RTU'd (Returned to Unit) because they didn't have the facilities there to help me, I had a pretty good idea that this was some kind of depression or PTSD type thing but didn't know a lot about either of these things really wanted someone to confirm my thinking. I'd searched the symptoms of depression on the internet and as I worked my way through the list, one by one I ticked most of them off and figured that I was probably suffering depression. I was aware my issues only really started after Afghan, I looked up the symptoms of PTSD, again I worked my way through the list. Emotional numbness? Check. Quick to anger? Check. Becoming stressed or destressed if reminded of certain events? Check. Nightmares of certain events in your past? Check. I didn't have any flashbacks and the websites I looked at said a person must be directly involved with a traumatic event to have PTSD. I wasn't, so I figured this wasn't me, it was a coincidence.

I felt massively relieved that I'd told somebody about what was going on, but I also felt like the biggest bullshitter in the history of all bullshit. I constantly told myself 'You're just trying to get time off', 'There's nothing wrong with you' and 'There's guys out there that are much more deserving of this treatment than you, you're just wasting everyone's time'. That last one is an absolute classic with forces lads going through a mental shit storm and is a prime example of why your own brain can be the biggest bellend you've ever known because it will try to convince you that you don't need or deserve any help at a time when the help is what you need more than ever. It's seriously good at doing this. This thought stayed with me for years after, because what caused my issues (being an outside observer of lots of death and injury) wasn't what I'd normally associate with the cause of depression or PTSD. I've met lads who dragged half of their mate out of a building after a grenade blast or witnessed their mate take a round through the side of the chest. That's the type of shit I'd associate with PTSD so who the fuck was I to even consider that this what was going on here?

This took me years and a shit load of therapy to get over but for now, sat in this temporary med centre, at our glorified camp site, I felt like the biggest fraud in the world. Within 3 hours they had a car down come to collect me. I loaded my stuff into it, with the help of some of the guys I'd been working with at the Olympics. I spent the next 4-hour journey back to RAF Leeming stewing in my own sense of failure and imposter syndrome, questioning my decision to talk to someone and whether or not I would still have a job in a few months.

Chapter 13

I don't deserve to be here

'Durka Durka Mohammed Jihad' is not a suitable drill cadence

The day after getting back to my unit I was in the med centre seeing the doc, I don't remember much about this other than it was pretty short, it ended up with them referring me onto the military mental health guys known as DCHM which stands for 'Department of Community Mental Health'. I went back to work after that expecting things to happen pretty quickly. Nope. 3 weeks it took them to see me, that's 3 weeks of not being able to answer the questions asked by my Chain of Command about why I was back from the Olympics early, what was wrong with me and what I could and couldn't do for work (which seemed pointless to me because we never really did anything). So, I just carried on as normal, feeling like a colossal fuck up and no idea what was going on. I was pretty open with my management, I told them what had been going on with my head recently and that I thought it was depression and, for the most part, they were OK with it, they made the right noises 'If you need anything just ask', 'Keep us up to date' etc but I didn't tell them about what had gone on in Afghan because I still refused to believe that any of that could be causing this and if it was that shit then I felt embarrassed that something as stupid and insignificant as that (remember that part about your head being a dick? Yeah) could have caused this. I was asked plenty of times 'What's caused this?', 'Why are you depressed?' as if I knew and even if I did know as if I'd just be able to rattle it off like it was a fucking takeaway order; "I'll take 13 IED blasts, 7 gunshot wounds, 3 mine blasts and an extra portion of charred child corpse'.

Once my DCMH appointment finally came around, I drove over to Catterick (the nearest military quack clinic to us) and sat in the waiting room. I was nervous about what was going to happen, my sense of imposter syndrome was bigger than ever. I looked around at the other guys in the waiting room and manufactured stories as to why they were there. Thinking of the most horrific shit that they'd been through, all infinitely better reasons than mine to be there, I thought about walking out at one point. The idea that I would tell this shrink everything that had happened, and they'd sit there saying 'Yeah but why are you here?' became a very real probability in my head.

Let me just pause there for a second because this is a really important point that I want to get across to folks reading this. When I say your head is a dick and can fuck you up, I mean it. It will try it's best to bully you and make you believe things that are total horseshit, it will do everything in its power to stop you getting the help you need and it's a pro at this. It will lie to you; tell you that it's hopeless, you're useless and don't deserve the help or can't be helped. So, I've got one very simple rule when it comes to mental health stuff. You know fuck all about what's going on inside your own head. That's it. If you're at a point where you don't feel quite right in your head, you're acting out of the ordinary or your view of yourself or the world has drastically changed for the worse then speak to the doc. In the first instance speaking to a mate or family member is fucking brilliant, do it, its mind blowing what a difference that can make but at some point down the line you're going to need to hand this over to the professionals to get you squared away. Once you've started that ball rolling then let them deal with it and go along for the ride. Chances are your brain will fight you along the way, tell it to shut the fuck up and carry on getting help because your brain can't be trusted, and you know nothing about what's happening up in there. Mental health isn't just 'feeling sad' or being 'crazy' it's a physical issue in your head that's either causing chemicals getting released in the wrong amounts or the connections in your brain aren't firing like they should be. Unless you're trained in that shit then you have no place in deciding whether or not you deserve to be sitting in that waiting room.

Anyway, eventually my wait was up, I walked in to see the shrink, A young RAF mental health nurse (who, incidentally, was pretty fit, making it harder to focus on my noggin rather than her chest). We sat and exchanged pleasantries for a while I was trying to second guess her analysing my every answer and waiting for the inevitable 'tell me about your childhood' question which came and went without any major 'holy shit' type of breakthrough, the 'are you planning on killing yourself?' question came and went (3rd time I've been asked this so far). I was waiting for my que to get down to the nitty gritty and tell my story about why I was there, but it never came. After 45 minutes of nothing particularly meaty that was it and we got another session booked in for 2 weeks later. Even more frustrating was that I still didn't have a diagnosis or any better understanding of what was going on. Turns out this first session is more about building a rapport and trust with each other, to me it felt like a waste of time but knowing what I know now from my coaching work (more on this later) it's actually a vital part of the process. Put it this way, you're not likely to sit down with someone who you've never met before and start telling them all your deepest, darkest secrets and what is likely the worst parts of your life (apart from those weird people who will tell you about their messy divorce and problems in the bedroom 10 minutes after meeting you. If you're one of those people pack it in! It's fucking weird!). They also got me to fill in a bunch of questionnaires. Each one asked questions around different areas, depression, anxiety, trauma/stress and alcohol habits. My depression and trauma score were pretty high, my anxiety score was average and alcohol score low (I didn't drink much anymore). These questionnaires were repeated every time I had an appointment. The scores would stay roughly the same unless I was going through a particularly good or really shitty time. They seemed to put a lot of weight on the scores and how the session would play out would seem to depend heavily on my scores in these tests. These would become known as my 'mental tests'.

Before my first session had even started, I planned to make a stop off at McDonalds on my way back to base after it had finished as I expected some mentally exhausting ordeal that would take time and greasy food to process properly. I never had the ordeal but still stopped for a burger, this became a habit after every session as a little 'reward' for another session done. What it actually became was a habit of comfort eating every time I had to face up to my mental head. It started with a takeaway after each session and snowballed into devouring whatever the cholesterol filled piece of goodness that I could get my hands on any time the opportunity presented itself. This became so deeply engrained that I went from about 13 stone of largely bone, organs and muscle to 18 stone of largely doughnuts, biscuits and chocolates. A lot of folks turn to alcohol to numb the pain caused by a messed-up head, I tried that, but it didn't work, I just felt worse. Some folks turn to drugs but that just never appealed to me, others turn to self-harm. I tried that as well by cutting myself but that just fucking hurt! So, I numbed the pain with food, a fucking boat load of it.

Over the next couple of months, the 2nd and 3rd sessions got a little more in depth, I got to tell the 'story' of what happened in Afghan, she asked me a few questions about how I felt at the time and how I felt when I got home but we didn't go much deeper than that. My memory of this period isn't great so I don't know if I either down played everything because it was too painful to bring up in all its fucked-up detail or if my brain had started to hide away the shittiest stuff, but I never felt like I really got across things as well as I could have. Maybe this is why when I finally asked Miss fit nurse to give me an actual diagnosis. During our 4th session I was shocked when she told me 'I think this a case of low mood'. Low mood? What the fuck!? Now, I could be wrong, but to me low mood is 'I've been feeling a bit shit lately' not 'I feel completely empty, I can't feel any emotion other than anger, I'm starting fights with random people who would pulverise me and I can't stop thinking about people being killed in Afghan'. She explained that low mood is a type of minor depression and said if I felt like I needed them, I could start taking anti-depressants to help.

I was starting to get pissed off, after 5 sessions I didn't feel like we'd actually done any work to try and help me deal with my issues and we'd only spoken about Afghan stuff at a surface level. Once, maybe twice, I turned down her offer of anti-depressants because I knew that if people in the military started them, they were instantly medically downgraded. This is a military term that basically means going long term sick but in the majority of cases a person could do their normal job, just not do certain things affected by their medical condition. This could be anything from an ingrown toe nail to a broken back; it also included mental health stuff. But to me this felt like signing the death certificate on my career in the forces and I wasn't willing to risk this just 3 years into it. Aside from not feeling like I was getting any treatment I was still pissed off with this diagnosis of 'low mood' which lead to some interesting conversations with my management back on camp who were as eager as ever to know what was going on with me. By this time my CoC had started 'requesting' (I had no choice) regular meetings with me to check on my welfare. These started out nice enough, if a little pointless. They'd ask how I was doing, if I needed anything, try in some weird, roundabout way, to find out what was going on in my head using psychology gained from years of watching TV.

After another couple of sessions, I felt shitter than I ever had done and like I was getting nowhere fast so I decided to take up the offer of medication because the way I was going I felt like I wouldn't have a job soon anyway. They started me on 10mg of Citalopram, a really common anti-depressant that's supposed to increase your levels of serotonin (one of your 'feel good' chemicals), a few weeks down the line and I felt no different, so they upped it to 20mg. After a few weeks on this I was starting to feel a bit better and my mental tests scores were lower meaning I was less mental, my shrink took this as I was all good and discharged me.

Now here's the thing, anti-depressants are designed to make depression (and other conditions like it) feel less shitty so you're in a better place to start working on what's caused things to get fucked up. They don't cure the condition. It's a bit like giving someone with a dislocated ankle a strong painkiller, they'll be in less pain, but the ankle is still dislocated, and it will probably stay that way until a professional sorts it out. Also, mental health isn't one big shitty slide downwards, it's more of a roller coaster of times that aren't so bad, and things feel better and times that are really bad diarrhoea type shittyness. So, if you've put someone on anti-depressants, given it a few weeks and they turn up saying 'yeah I'm feeling pretty good' that doesn't mean things are squared away and everything is fine, especially if you haven't done any actual therapy to sort out the root cause. Now, I'm not a professional in mental health so I'm happy to be told I'm wrong, but to me it makes perfect sense. Take the edge off, treat the root cause, create a plan for the person to use if things go south again.

I stayed on the anti-depressants for a few weeks after getting discharged from DCMH and then on the doctors' orders gradually came off them until I was completely off. I was chuffed to bits. I'd beaten it! And it wasn't so bad after all, I didn't even have to talk about any of the painful stuff in much detail or challenge any of the beliefs I'd formed about it all.

Chapter 14

Man up

My Flight Sergeant did not fight in the Crimean war and he does not remember what it was like in Victorian times

You could stop reading this now and think 'This is the shittest book about mental health ever!' but you've probably guessed by now, that wasn't the end of my trouble, far from it.

After about 4 months I was back in front of the doctor in the med centre telling him how I felt low, hopeless, didn't enjoy anything, still couldn't feel any emotions and was angry at the world, all the same shit as I was having before. Back onto the Citalopram and another 3 weeks wait and back off to DCMH I went. Hand on heart, I don't remember any of my appointments around this time, I'm pretty sure I saw the same fit mental health nurse as before who then sent me on to a psychiatrist, but I don't remember a single thing about him. It was at this time that I was diagnosed with depression rather than this 'low mood' bullshit, it was a small win but maybe it meant I'd finally start getting some proper treatment (it didn't). While DCMH were going through the motions things at work were getting really fucked up. My CoC were getting tired of me being ill, every time I had an appointment I had to answer a shit load of questions to justify why it needed to be in work time and why I couldn't do guard or parade (remember when I said about downgrading meaning you couldn't do certain things, well anti-depressants is an automatic 'no access to weapons' and 'no going on tour'). My weekly meetings with my sergeant started to get shitty and they now consisted of me sitting in front of 2 or 3 Senior NCO's or officers having to justify to them why I had a couple of days off sick last week (usually because I was seriously worried I'd do something dumb to myself or somebody else or because I simply couldn't face the prospect of not crying in bed and having to face people). At this time, we had an Army 2nd Lieutenant in charge of our squadron (fuck knows why as we're an RAF unit) who looked 18, talked like he was 16 and had the intelligence of a 12-year-old and would step on his own gran to get promoted, this guy was a grade A arse nugget. He decided to start sitting in on our little meetings and every now and then would interject with his little gems of advice like:

2nd LT *"So is everything OK with your family?"*

Me *"yes"*

2nd LT *"And everything is OK in your relationship?"*

Me *"yes"* (Kel was still as rock solid as ever)

2nd LT *"What about finances, is everything OK with money?"*

Me *"yes"*

2nd LT *"So can't you just wake up and like, be happy?"*

Or the classic

"I know life in the forces can be tough sometimes and we can all find it hard but it's times like that when you just need to man up and crack on"

This brings me nicely to my next rant. I fucking hate 'Man up', there's not many more phrases out there that are as stupid or potentially damaging as 'man up'. I'm not going to bang on about masculinity or gender identities, you can identify as a pineapple for all I care, and I'm not talking about someone throwing a hissy fit because it's too cold or complaining about being tired while on ops, in that case you probably should toughen up a bit, at least until the job is done. What I'm talking about is telling someone to man up who is going through a genuinely tough time or is in pain. Telling somebody who's genuinely suffering to man up is basically telling them to not talk about their suffering and act like everything is fine. Blokes especially, are a nightmare for doing this without any extra encouragement stopping them from talking to someone when they're going through a really shitty time. It's caused guys to take their own life because they didn't know what help was available because they never spoke to anyone about it or because they tried to talk to someone and were told to 'man up'. The military are particularly shit for doing this and there are times when it's suitable, but not many. Maybe just try not being a dick and listening to what someone is really saying before telling them to man up, you never know, you might save a life.

Anyway, back to business.

Life got pretty shit in general at this point, I was getting shit from my management, the guys on my section were getting pissed off with me getting time off sick and for med appointments and started making shitty little comments about me being 'mental' and about my increasing weight. Things were getting tough at home as well, Kel was having a really hard time living with me, she was still as supportive as ever, but I was basically a total nightmare to be around. Nothing ever brought me any joy or happiness, I didn't care about **anything** (and not in the 'I don't care what anyone thinks of me' bullshit. I literally didn't care about any one or anything and this isn't anywhere near as freeing or as cool as people make it out to be, it's actually a lonely as fuck mind-set), I didn't even care if I lived or died anymore. The only things I did care about were Kel and Meg, our cute as fuck Border Collie puppy we got shortly after getting married. She was a rescue dog who had a tough start to life. She had a lot of issues when we took her in and it took a lot of time and training to settle her down and help her trust us. Not only was she a ball of fluffiness but she was dependant on me to keep her fed, walked, constantly entertained (if you've ever owned a collie you'll know what I mean), this forced me to get off my arse and do something, even if it's as small as take a dog for a walk or feed it, it gave my life a small glimpse of purpose and meaning. She also makes me laugh every single day and anything that can make someone who's depressed laugh is always a winner. Without Meg (and Kel of course) I genuinely don't think I'd be here now,

I'd probably be imprinted on a lamp post on the side of a motorway somewhere.

One of the hardest parts of my illness was the total lack of feeling, I once had a conversation with Kel which involved me telling her that although I knew that I did love her, I didn't feel love for her and that was fucking horrible. I didn't feel love or attachment to anything, least of all to myself. She really found it hard at this point because I was always so distant, so clinical, unfeeling and unaffectionate. I couldn't bare someone being so close as to give me a hug or a kiss. I'd dismiss any attempt at affection from her and brush it off as if it was a total stranger trying to hug me. Although not as severe, I still have this problem now, I find the idea of a long hug or someone being close to my face deeply uncomfortable. It's as if they're getting in my way of some unknown objective and how dare they try to give me affection when I'm trying to get something done? That's a work in progress.

I can't remember when it started but I also started having night terrors a few times a week. Obviously, I don't remember these because I was asleep but Kel would wake me up telling me that I was thrashing about in bed and shouting things like *"He's dead, he's fucking dead"*. I'd wake up out of breath, sometimes crying into my pillow and feeling like I'd just run a marathon. These got worse around major dates like remembrance Sunday, the dates I was in Afghan or if something reminded me that day of what had gone on over there like a movie or TV program. Whenever this happened, I'd feel like shit for putting Kel through it, I mean who wants to be woken up by something shouting about dead people and then crying in their pillow? Sometimes I would lie awake in bed, feeling tired enough to sleep but not wanting to sleep in case it happened again, putting myself and her through it.

On top of all this I was so low it began to feel as though I was in constant physical pain in my own head. This is something that many folks don't realise about depression; it can cause physical pain, especially when things get particularly bad. For me the pain felt like a dull ache at the base of my skull, at the top of my neck. It felt like somewhere between a migraine and neck ache. Life stopped meaning anything, I felt as though I'd lost my identity as a man and as a human being, I felt like an empty shell of a person. Each month I'd end up taking around a week off work because I couldn't face the outside world, normally the one thing I could manage was to take Meg for a walk, I couldn't even do that now, I had nothing left in me, my tank was completely empty. One time I sat on the sofa feeling completely worthless, staring at the TV but not actually watching it. After a couple of hours, I needed a piss, normally a person would automatically get up and go to the toilet, but this is an inbuilt self-preservation thing. When you don't see any point in preserving yourself you don't do the things you normally would. So, I pissed myself sitting on the sofa, I sat on a soaking wet sofa for a couple of hours until eventually I managed to get myself cleaned up and wash the sofa. The only reason I did this is because I didn't want Kel to see me like this. I didn't tell her about this for months and I've only ever told a couple of people about this since. Although things would get worse (Spoiler alert!), this is what I consider as when I was at the **bottom of the barrel**.

I can't speak for anyone else, but I think this is the mindset people get in when they become suicidal. They have no attachment to their own life or anyone else, they feel like a burden on other people in their own life and they're in constant pain. Life stops meaning anything and it feels as there's no other way to stop the suffering. If you haven't started getting help by this point this is when shit gets really dangerous because you can't see any other way out of this shit storm, and you can't any light at the end of the tunnel. Neither did I for a while but I kept telling myself that things will eventually get better, and it won't last forever, nothing lasts forever, including the bad times so that means at some point, it will pass. I didn't believe it, but I kept telling myself it and this is what kept me going.

While writing this book I spoke to Twitch (I mentioned him at the start as one of my proof readers and subject matter experts about military and mental health matters). Here's what he had to say about his experience of suicide.

"When I attempted suicide, I didn't give a single thought for my loved ones, I only wanted the pain and flashbacks to stop. Once I made the decision to do it I felt strangely calm and remember feeling relieved as I drank the bottle of whiskey in maybe 3 or 4 gulps then methodically taking the pills, I remember feeling myself drift off and deciding to lay on the floor so I wasn't found upside down if I fell off the bed.......I woke up covered in vomit and piss thinking I was dead, I laid there for maybe hours staring at the light fitting waiting for someone to find me. It was morning when I stood up and began to cry...This was the moment I was re-born and began a new life without knowing how the fuck I had survived."

Listening to Twitch talk about his experience of attempting suicide was a really powerful thing. He's right as well, when you're in that mindset, ending your life makes perfect sense and feels like the only solution to what's going on. The thing with suicide is that it doesn't end the suffering, it only ends the prospect that things will get better. And if you take nothing else away from this entire book, just take this; it **WILL** get better. Pain and suffering are both finite, they do end, but it won't end by taking your own life. Like I said earlier, your brain is lying to you, there is hope and you **CAN** fight this.

Chapter 15

Faking it

SAC White must not insist he can sort out the 'Ruskies' with only a bandana and a knife

Before we get going with the next chapter, I think we should have another dumb story because this book isn't about to lighten up any time soon. Short one this time though.

I was 19 and doing the usual thing of making my way around the bars trying to find any young lady that was drunk enough to think that I was good looking enough to go back to hers. After a particularly heavy night I managed to find a lass who took a liking to me, she was in her 30's, I was 19, WINNER! This was before Netflix even existed, so we went back to hers for 'coffee', we had a quality night together, she taught me some stuff and I thought she was gorgeous.

We agreed to meet up for a proper date a week later and met at her local pub, wanting to be a gent I turned up early and sat there waiting for her. Eventually some random bird walks up to me, talking to me as if she knew me. She sat herself down opposite me and took a sip out of the drink I'd bought for my date. After a couple of minutes trying to figure out what was going on and who this cheeky bint was it dawned on me. The cheeky bint was my date, I was so smashed the first time I met her that in my mind she was a completely different person, like looking through super strength beer goggles. The lass in my mind was an easy 8/10 and the lass sat in front of me was a generous 4/10, but not one to judge a book by its cover I stuck around and figured I'd at least enjoy a drink with her.

As the night wore on it wasn't going great, something was wrong, and I couldn't put my finger on it. I knew she wasn't a looker but then again, I'm not exactly a model. After a while it dawned on me, this lass was bat shit crazy. And not the kind of crazy I'm talking about in this book, like shave your body hair to create a shrine of you then slash your tires type of crazy. Now this would have been easy if she wasn't enjoying it either, but she was having a great time in her own little bat-shit crazy world. Thankfully I had a plan. I'd text my best mate Simo (remember the dodgy poem in my last story? Yeah, him) asking him to rescue me. I told him to park outside the pub and call me acting like something was wrong at home and he'd come to pick me up to take me back sharpish. Well after 15 minutes he was good as gold and turned up like I asked, but rather than waiting outside he came in, tripped on the way in, making sure every bastard in that boozer knew he was there, sat at the table with me and my psycho date. He said he'd come to get me like I asked making it perfectly clear to psycho lass that I'd asked to be rescued. I didn't even try to salvage this, I got up and walked out. It took months of ignoring messages and calls to finally shake her.

Anyway, back to the grind.

I finally got a break in work when I was added to a specialist team tasked with bringing in a brand-new comms platform called FALCON. This was a billion-pound project that would be rolled out across the entire MOD and would provide the comms backbone for all deployments in the future and my team was in charge of working it out and bringing it into service for the RAF. My health was still fucked but I finally had something to keep my mind busy, I didn't have time to think about all the shitty stuff and I was working with a great bunch of lads. The management was pretty decent, and it was good, honest graft. We started doing shifts, going on exercises and grafting, I finally got a taste of the military that I joined up for. What's even better, I was good at it and we had a CoC (Chain of Command, in case you've forgotten) who supported us and encouraged us to improve. This was when I worked out that although I had a lot of my own shit to work out with the docs a lot of my feelings that were so shit all the time came from the toxic conditions at work. I had no escape from my mind, I would come from home where I had all the time in the world to think of my issues and walk into work where I had even more time to be in my own fucked up head and have to deal with shitty management.

I did this job for a year and while it had its tough parts I loved it, my work finally meant something, and I was making a real difference with my job. Unfortunately, we all did such a bang-up job that it was now ready to hand over to the other comms squadrons to take into service.

This meant going back to my normal Squadron, with the shower of wankers in there and the place where I know my head gets really fucked up. I was shitting myself, and with good cause.

Back on squadron, my sergeants were watching my every move, both in and out of work. And they were sneaky little bastards, on a couple of occasions I was pulled in the office and asked why I was at a restaurant with Kel when I was off work. Apparently, if I could go out for a meal with the Mrs it couldn't possibly mean that I was actually depressed. When anyone is signed off sick in the military it's usually with certain criteria, such as 'must not leave base' or 'must not sky dive without parachute'. Most of the time my conditions were always 'sick in quarters' which is military speak for I was able to stay at home and do whatever I needed to do to get better. They were following my social media and when Kel tagged us having a meal somewhere it meant that I was breaking these conditions because I wasn't in my house. They seriously expected me to spend the entire time I was off sick in my house and this would somehow help?

Things blew up one day when I was called into their office, my sergeant and my flight sergeant were both sat there and told me to sit down. They had a bunch of sick chits on the desk (sick chit is a military term for doctors note). They both spoke softly and told me that they didn't want to upset me (they were treading seriously carefully, I imagine because they knew what they were about to do was seriously wrong). They said they had concerns over the amount of time I was taking off, the amount of taskings in work I was missing and how the guys on the squadron felt about me. Apparently, people were getting pissed off with me being off work, not only this but they said that every time I was off work (because my head was so fucked, I couldn't face the world) it coincided with when a tasking needed to be done. In other words, I was faking my illness to get out of work. I couldn't believe what I was hearing, I told them that I spent most of my time looking for work when I was in rather than avoiding it, none of the guys on my section had said anything to me about getting pissed off. Somehow, I managed to keep my cool, didn't get upset and didn't throw a chair at them. I just told them that this isn't something that I would just fake to get out of doing shit at work and if they thought I was faking it they would need to take that up with the docs who had decided to give me this time off (90% of the time I was given off sick was suggested by the doc rather than asked for by me). We went on for a while with them trying to convince me to admit too them that I was faking the whole thing in what felt like an interrogation. They wanted me to agree that I'd take less time off and would take part with squadron stuff more. The meeting finished with nothing agreed, I walked out, jumped on my bike and rode home.

On my way home something odd happened, I felt something weird deep inside me, it was like an urgency of 'I need to get home now!', I felt like I had to get away from everyone as soon as possible but I didn't know why. I rode as quick as I could and ditched my bike in the garden and got inside the house. As soon as I got in I my breathing got became rapid, I couldn't control it, I got dizzy and was absolutely shitting myself. I had no fucking idea what was going on but it as scary as hell. I kept running through that meeting in my head over and over again, I couldn't think straight, I was hysterically crying (I promise I don't normally cry as much as this book makes out, I was in a pretty bad place but hey, if as a dude you feel like shedding a tear will help then cry away, everyone cries sometimes). Everything felt like it was moving a thousand miles an hour. Looking back, I think I was having some sort of panic attack along with a mental breakdown, things were properly screwed up and I had no idea what I was doing. Suddenly the anger and hatred enveloped me, I couldn't believe they pulled this shit and I wanted to show them that I was genuinely ill. The only way I could think of doing this was to hurt myself in the way that a mentally well person would never do. I remembered that I had a Colt 1911 air pistol under my bed that I kept for plinking stuff in the garden and figured that if I shot myself with it that this would prove that I really was fucked in the head, I could show them an actual physical wound to prove them wrong (When you're having a full blown breakdown you think and do shit that make no logical sense).

I went upstairs and got the pistol out from its case, loaded a few of the metal pellets and CO_2 into the magazine and loaded the pistol, I cocked the slide back and my first instinct was to put it in my mouth but after a few seconds of the muzzle sitting in my mouth I figured that this was pointless, they would never see the wound, I needed something to show them. I figured I'd shoot myself in the arm, that would be nice and obvious. I took the safety off and pressed the muzzle against my arm. Something stopped me from pulling the trigger, it felt like I was on the verge of completely giving up. I stopped and considered whether I was ready to do this; To completely throw in the towel and accept my fate. It felt like if I did this one act of hurting myself, things would surely snowball into something much worse. This thought distracted me for just long enough to realise that was I was doing was pretty dumb and if those wankers at work wouldn't take me seriously by now then planting a metal ball bearing a few centimetres in my arm wasn't going to change anything. I dropped the gun and slumped by the bed, still hyper ventilating, shaking like a shitting dog and unable to make sense of anything around me. I still really wanted to hurt myself in some way, it was the only thing I could think of and it made perfect sense. I thought about different ways people hurt themselves, I thought about cutting myself, pouting boiling water on myself, throwing myself in front of a car, even full on suicide. Suddenly I heard what seemed like a little voice shouting up from the shit storm inside my mind, "What the fuck are you doing!? Get some help!". I realised that I was about to just throw in the towel and let everything I had fought against win.

I thought 'No, fuck this. Fuck them, I won't let them win. I have no idea how, but I can do this, there's something we haven't tried and that will be the key to getting me squared away. Right now, though I need to get help'. My first thought was to call one of the lads on my squadron who I got on well with, he knew that I'd been having a shitty time and he'd be willing to help me. I called him but only got a voicemail message, I left a message and sent him a text telling him to come around because I was in a shit state. Not knowing how long it would take him to respond (it was 45 minutes before he called me back). Rather than wait for him I decided to call Kel who was at the vets for a routine appointment with Meg. She took the call while in the waiting room, instantly recognising that something was seriously wrong she got in the car and drove home. Like the legend that she is Kel kept me on the phone the entire way home I couldn't talk much because I was breathing like something possessed but I managed to get out something like 'work... faking it... need help' but she got the idea and came home sharpish. When she got home I was huddled up on the sofa, I didn't even register that she was there for 5 minutes. Just sat, curled up, hyper-ventilating, crying, staying into the abyss. After a while I calmed down and managed to tell her what had gone on, she hit the fucking roof and wanted to storm into work and have a screaming match. Knowing that this wouldn't help anything it was my turn to calm her down now.

The next day there was no way I could face the guys in work, after what had happened the day before. It was pretty clear that I was a danger to myself and needed to get something sorted rapid. I went straight to the docs in the morning and explained what had happened, both in the meeting and when I got home. It's probably safe to say the doc was pretty pissed as well and said they'd deal with it internally (no idea what happened here, probably nothing) but insisted that there was no way I was fit to work and signed me off for a couple of weeks. This crushed me because although she was right in my mind this was playing right into their hands and would only make it worse. The cruel part was that whenever you're signed off sick you need take a copy of the sick chit into work and hand it to your management, the same management who had just accused me of using sick chits to get out of work. Not really having a choice in this I went into work and found the sergeant who led the meeting the day before and handed it to him without saying anything. He looked at it and then back at me, the first thing he said was "Are you making out that this is to do with what we spoke about last night?" What a colossal cock juggling thunder twat.

I told him that it wasn't just to avoid the shitty conversation that was going to follow and to reduce the chances of me doing I would later regret and walked out. The next couple of weeks saw me having more DCMH and docs appointments and between us it was decided that it would be better for me if I was posted away from Leeming to somewhere else and make a fresh start. My health had only gotten worse while I was there and things had gotten so bad in work, I couldn't face being in that environment anymore. They sorted out this sudden move using a pretty rare posting type called a 'medical geographical posting' which translated in normal person speak means 'For the sake of his health, get this guy away from there and somewhere better for him'. I'd already been at Leeming for 5 years of what was meant to be a 4-year posting; so this was fine in my books and quite frankly I couldn't wait to get away from there.

Within 3 weeks the paperwork was signed off, me and Kel had packed up our house and we were on the road down to RAF Cosford near Wolverhampton. I only told a few of the guys from work I was leaving, I felt bad about it, but I wanted to completely cut ties from that place and start fresh.

Chapter 16

A fresh start

SAC White must not put up posters comparing my sergeant to Peter Griffin. Even if he really does look like him.

It was no accident that I got Cosford as a posting. It was close to Kels family (after spending years close to mine), it was in a decent part of the country and by all accounts the work there was pretty chilled out meaning I could focus on getting myself sorted out but with actual work to do. Rather than spending years sitting on my arse achieving nothing and it was far away from my old base, the place I associated all my troubles with, it felt like the perfect place for a fresh start.

I was to work at the training school where they taught the new guys from my trade group. My job was basically to fix any IT shit that broke from amongst the 300 odd computers, servers, projectors etc. It wasn't glamorous, it wasn't exciting, and it wasn't the big impact I wanted to make, but it was decent, somewhat skilled work with a decent team of lads. There were only 6 of us in the entire section and while I always said I hated the idea of working in the office it dawned on me that's pretty much what I'd spent the last 5 years doing so I figured I'd just embrace it and make the most of it.

For all the positives of this new posting, this was a far cry from what I expected from a career in the military. I had deployed twice, one of those times was in the UK, I'd been on exercise 3 times which mostly consisted of being cold, wet and fucking miserable rather than running around playing soldier, I hadn't seen any of the camaraderie or brotherhood you see in the media or recruitment ads portray. Now I was a low-level computer tech (albeit a well-paid one) in what I was now sure would be my last few months in the military before they booted me out for being a massive burden on the system. I was still diagnosed with depression and nobody seemed to know why I hadn't miraculously got better, no matter what drugs they gave me or which therapist I spoke to. I was certain that I was suffering from PTSD. The symptoms I'd read about back in 2012 weren't just still there, they were worse. A day didn't go by where I didn't think about that time in Afghan, anything that reminded me of Afghan made me deeply uncomfortable at best and sent me into a downward spiral of darkness at worst. Seeing a Jackal or a Mastiff driving out on the roads, seeing an Apache helicopter flying overhead, even seeing a hearse was shit because it reminded me of the guys who hadn't been lucky enough to make it back alive landing at RAF Lyneham and driving through Wootton Bassett. It was like I'd become super aware of anything that remotely linked to my time in Afghan and my brain clung to it.

As much as I didn't feel like I deserved a PTSD diagnosis, I was now convinced more than ever that I was suffering from the symptoms of it. The more I read up on it the more it made sense. Eventually I learned about complex PTSD (CPTSD), a form of the condition that came about from prolonged exposure to stress and trauma. Often victims of abuse, false imprisonment or members of the emergency services might be prone to this. As I read this everything seemed to click into place. Impulsive behaviour, difficulty maintaining relationships with people, alteration in self-perception, difficulty in identifying emotions. I ticked every box. I was given a new shrink, an ex-military psychologist. I told him about what I'd found but he wasn't interested. He said my PTSD symptoms were a side effect of my depression and I didn't have PTSD and he wouldn't entertain the idea of CPTSD. Maybe I didn't fit the mould of someone who would have PTSD; I'd never been shot at, I'd never directly witnessed a death or major injury, I'd had a good childhood. The military work on protocols and plans, I didn't fit any of their plans for what PTSD should look like and because of this they wouldn't even consider it and CPTSD is still pretty unrecognised. I tried to argue my case but who am I to tell a doc with more time in psychology than I'd been alive that he was wrong about this stuff? I knew that a diagnosis of PTSD was a death sentence on my career in the forces but by this point I was past caring. I just wanted all this to be over, whatever it took, either by me getting the proper treatment and accepting a future in civvy street or by me not being here anymore.

Although my knowledge of therapy was practically nil, Kel was a qualified therapist and was convinced I hadn't yet received any actual therapy to get my head sorted out, she felt like they were only dealing with surface level stuff and not addressing the root cause. I was feeling defeated, let down by the system that was there to help me, and I was continually having thoughts that I was a fraud, faking it, an attention seeker or trying to play the system, probably because that's what I had been told by my chain of command for the last few years. I was seething with anger about what had happened before I left Leeming, I obsessed over what they had said in that meeting, I constantly thought of ways to get revenge on them, everything from smearing shit on their cars to pushing them in front of traffic. I even wrote an email to each of them venting off all my hatred and anger, calling them every name under the sun and saved them as drafts, ready to send whenever my last day in the forces came around (I never got to send these, it was for the best). I developed a deep mistrust of anyone with the rank above Sergeant, I felt like they were all out to screw me over, they were all self-serving arseholes and couldn't be trusted.

This mistrust of senior ranks coupled with my total lack of giving a shit lead to some interesting conversations with senior ranks. We once had an Air Commodore come to see us, usually nobody really knew why these senior officers bothered to visit, I always suspected they got a kick out of knowing that everyone had to spend days cleaning every square inch of the base prior to their visit only for them to be an hour late and breeze through their visit not noticing or giving a shit how clean the back of the radiators were. This particular bloke came to see the lads in the IT section and one by one spoke to each of us. when he got around to me, he asked if I enjoyed my job. I think my answer of "Same shit different day but it pays the bills Sir" wasn't what he expected. I somehow managed to dodge the bullet with that one as well and not get in shit for it. I expect they knew it wasn't worth bollocking the mental guy.

My relationship with Kel was strained, and although we were experts at talking things through (seriously, this is key if you want a good relationship). I felt as though I was constantly pushing her away and like she was quietly regretting marrying me. My head was also doing it's best to convince me that she was part of the problem and I didn't love her anymore (again, more bullshit from my brain). I'd lost a load of mates by either losing touch with them or pushing them away to the point where they sacked me off. I didn't feel like I could talk to my folks about it because I would have to tell them what I thought was causing it all and I didn't want to do that for fear of it would be too painful for them to hear.

But maybe things would be different now, I had an opportunity to turn this around, new house, new job, new work mates and management, new mental health guys. Getting to Cosford was a breath of fresh air in what had been a few years of feeling like I was trudging uphill through thigh-deep mud, constantly hoping that things would be better if I kept going but it only got worse. Things got off to a solid start in my new job, I settled in to the new team quickly, I had work to keep me busy and if I finished that there was plenty more to do. I could get in some gym time pretty much whenever I wanted and Kel had a new job as a support worker in a school which she loved.

To distract myself and try to get some of my fitness back (because by this point, I had become a right porker) I started training for a half marathon. At Leeming I loved running and I did a couple of sponsored challenges on my own to raise money for charity, so this felt like a natural progression. I started training without any real plan, I just ran for a while, then the next run I'd go a bit further, and keep doing this. Looking back, I don't think this is how you train for a half marathon, but I felt good doing it, it got my mind off what had gone on before, and I could start to get my fitness back. However, in typical me fashion I pushed myself too hard and too quick. I Started to get shooting pains in my knee. I ignored this for a couple of months, figuring it was just usual pain from training and it would pass in its own time. After a while it got worse and I couldn't run due to the pain, so I decided to see the Doc. He told me that I had iliotibial band syndrome (no idea what this means, it just hurt like a bastard) and that it's unlikely I'll be doing any long distance runs any time soon. He sent me to see one of the physios to start getting sorted out.

This felt like a huge knock-back to me, I'd found something productive to do, for a good cause and it had nothing to do with mental health. I agreed to see the physio so I could get it sorted and start running again as soon as possible. On the day I first saw my physio my head was going a 100mph, this had become a common trait and it could either work for me or against me. Sometimes my brain would race thinking of all the shitty things that have happened, could happen, thinking of dead people or injuries and would usually result in a mental car crash where the dark clouds would gather. Other times my brain would think of ideas for businesses, inventions, TV programmes, books, get rich quick schemes (usually all bollocks) or I would pick a random subject and want to learn everything about it. Like how an engine works, what is quantum physics? (I still don't really know) or how to train a dog to dance? Although this was exhausting, I loved it because I felt excited and productive. On this day my brain had gone down the second route and I was hyper stimulated. Walking into the Physios treatment room I didn't hold back, I told him everything about everything, the issues with my head, the half marathon, about my wife, my dog, about Afghan. Although he was a military PT and was obviously really busy with other patients he patiently sat and smiled while I rambled on. After a while he stopped me and said, "I've just finished a book, I think you should read because it's perfect for someone like you, it's called '**7 habits of highly effective people**', I think you'll love it". I only half listened to him and started my rambling again, it was 25 minutes before we would even talk about my knee, but his suggestion planted a tiny seed in my mind that would later go on to change my life forever.

I was feeling a lot better in my head, my mood was better, and I felt ready to tackle this shit, despite the shrinks taking the same 'wait and see' approach as the previous ones, I felt good. My mental test scores were lower, and I felt positive, ready to tackle this shit. So, a month after I got to my new base, they discharged me from the mental health guys. Yup. Right at the point where I was ready to get my teeth into the root causes of my issues, I was deemed healthy enough to not need any further care. Maybe they had a point though? I mean who was I to argue with the professionals? Plus, I was feeling pretty good, maybe all I needed was this fresh start and a new work environment. Also, because Citalopram was useless for me, I was now on a high dose of Venlafaxine, another type of anti-depressant that seemed to be working well for me and levelled me out, maybe all this combined meant I was squared away?

Yeah, fucking right.

Initially I took this all clear from the docs as a win, a chance to move on from this shitty period of my life, work on my career and start a family with Kel. I was told I was better, so I thought I was! What does it matter that I still couldn't feel any emotion or even describe to someone how I was feeling because I didn't know? It was fine that my watching videos of people from sandy places getting killed was now a full-blown hobby in which I'd lie in bed and piss myself laughing watching them die to pass the time. It's normal to loathe anyone who was a middle eastern fighting-aged male, profile people walking past me in the street to make sure they're not a terrorist and start making mental plans to fly back into Kandahar airport or Syria, buy a gun from the local market and go kill people who I thought were insurgents. I mean doesn't every short, fat, IT techy do that shit? I mean they'd taught me to shoot at stationary cardboard targets 100 yards away in my career, so I definitely knew what I was doing right? I was also becoming an arm chair expert in tactics, methods and equipment used by terrorists and counter terrorist agencies. Every terrorist attack (and there were a lot, this was the peak of ISIS being a bunch of colossal knob jockeys) would prompt me to learn about every detail of the attack, what weapons did they use? How did they plan the attack? How did they execute it? What did or should the authorities have done to prevent or counter it?

Yeah it was all good.

A few months in and things were going well at work, I'd quickly become established as the 'go to guy' to get shit done, the work I was putting out was bang on and I was getting praise from the higher ups. I felt competent and confident in my job and I actually enjoyed going to work. Things at home were improving as well, they were far from perfect but because my mood was better this had a knock-on effect with Kel. She didn't have to come home to seeing her husband sitting there in his pants, miserable as sin, a void expression on his face, stinking because he hadn't washed in a week. But I couldn't shake this awareness that I still couldn't feel anything. Even when my best mate handed me his new baby boy to hold, I felt nothing. If me and Kel went out for the day, I knew I had to say that I enjoyed it because nothing went wrong but I didn't feel any enjoyment, I just knew the right words to say. The docs had asked me to gradually reduce my medication and I'd just finished my last week on them, I figured maybe it was the meds dulling the emotions? Maybe I had to re-learn emotions? Maybe it would just take time. I tried to think of every excuse I could as to why my head still wasn't right. I gave it a month to see if things got squared away but they didn't. I wasn't even paying any attention to all the other fucked up stuff that was going on, I genuinely didn't think any of that was out of the ordinary, it was this emotion thing that concerned me. After putting it off for a bit longer, I decided to go back to the doc. I didn't want to go back to the shrinks, but I was hoping for some kind of magic medication or trick the doc could give me to start feeling again. To date, I'd spent so much time talking to docs about my head that it wasn't a big deal anymore. I could reel it off like I was reading a story, but this time it felt harder. It felt as though I was admitting that I wasn't fine, despite them telling me that I was and me wanting it to be true so much. Despite my best efforts to hold it back I blubbed like a baby in front of him, I felt like I'd failed at getting better, I felt like I'd let everyone down, the docs, Kel, my family and friends. Everyone wanted me to be fine and I couldn't do it. I told the doc that I would give anything to be able to feel happiness again. He listened to me for a while, looking at me as though I was telling him what I had for dinner last night. When I finished, he sighed and said "*So what is it exactly you want me to do?*" I thought 'Are you shitting me!?'. I've just sat here, poured my heart out, told him everything that had gone on and he was talking to me as though I was asking him to give me a 10-inch cock and the ability to shoot rainbows out my nipples! I tried my best to explain to him that I wanted help to feel emotions again, but he still seemed to think I was taking the piss. He told me to give it 2 weeks and then go back to him if I still felt the same way. Because, you know, 4 years of this shit is likely to change in 2 weeks.

I left that appointment and went back to work, but suddenly I wasn't feeling the same sense of eagerness to graft, I wasn't happy to be there, and I didn't want to see or speak to any of the lads on my section. I felt like I did back at Leeming, despondent, pissed off at the RAF, like they didn't give a shit about me, so I wouldn't give a shit about them. I even got caught out lying by one of the corporals on the section. By this point I made it a personal value of mine to never lie, not only was I terrible at it but I hated liars, even if it was going to get me in the shit, I'd tell the truth. I believed that if a person couldn't be trusted to tell the truth they're not worth bothering about. But in my pissed off mindset things started to slip. I sacked off a menial clerical task in favour of the gym and signed off the paperwork to say that I'd done it. It was a 6-hour long job that was done every week without fail and I seemed to be the only person who cared about it. Unknown to me, my corporal had decided to check that it was done on the same day that I'd signed it off as done. He'd noticed that it hadn't and asked me if I'd done it, I told him I had. It was a small lie and in the bigger picture it was fairly petty and inconsequential and writing this now it feels silly, but it was a major breach of trust. Liars aren't tolerated in the forces; how can you trust the guy next to you when the chips are down if he can't be trusted when everything is plane sailing? As soon as the words left my mouth, I knew I'd fucked up. He presented me with the evidence that I was talking bollocks and I came clean. He told me that he had no choice but to write me up and put me forward for a punishment. If it was someone that I didn't like I wouldn't have cared as much but this guy was a good lad, a grafter, great banter and looked after the guys under him. I didn't give a shit about the punishment and looking back the whole thing seems incredibly minor but to lie to a mate like that made me feel like a piece of dirt. Because of my good performance up until this point the punishment was minor (I don't remember what it was) but that betrayal of trust made me realise that I wasn't myself.

I floated through the next 2 weeks in neutral before my next appointment to see the doctor again. I hoped that it would be a different doctor this time and that they would listen to me and actually do something, but it wasn't. It was the same wanker as before. I sat down and told him that nothing had changed since the last time I saw him. He looked at me in the same way he did the first time, as if I was a burden on his day, an inconvenience sat in his office. He told me he would refer me back to DCMH again and to wait for an appointment letter. I waited 3 weeks for that letter to come through, when it did it said that I had an appointment to see the psychiatrist again but this time I would have to wait for 6 weeks before I could. By this point I could feel the rest of my symptoms coming back, the looming dark cloud, the fuzziness in my head, the feeling of emptiness and lack of identity. When things with my head got bad, I always felt like my brain was made of glass, but something had shattered the glass, a storm was blowing the shards of glass all over the place while I frantically tried to get the pieces back together again. I could feel that storm on the horizon, I was heading back down the rabbit hole and there was nothing I could do to stop it.

Chapter 17

Being an arsehole

'It wasn't me! You can't prove it!' is a bad response to
any senior rank calling my name

I couldn't wait those 6 weeks, I felt like the darkness had
completely enveloped me, I was miserable and all I could
feel was anger. I genuinely believed that everyone was an
arsehole until they proved me wrong, nobody could be
trusted except my wife and my dog. I went out my way
to be a dick to people, either losing my rag with people
in person or starting heated arguments with random
people online. I often fantasised about hurting people,
even randomly taking a swing for a random, innocent
person sitting in front of me. Many times, these fantasies
turned darker when I would play out a scenario in my
mind in which I'd somehow have a terrorist or an
insurgent kneeling down in front of me, me having a
pistol pointed at their head and relishing in the
opportunity to pull the trigger and rid the world of one
less bad guy. I knew this was pure fantasy, this wasn't
Hollywood, I'm not some movie hero and I've never
killed anyone. But I would still obsess over this scenario
and I found comfort in the prospect of killing someone.
Everywhere I went I would consider different horrific
scenario's and how they would pan out. A mass
shooting, a bomb, a knife attack. Everywhere I went I
would identify cover points, escape routes, makeshift
weapons, I'd play out the whole scenario in my head,

usually resulting in me saving the day and getting to kill the bad guy, again, relishing in the opportunity. It's as if my mind wanted an opportunity to make a real difference in the fight of good and evil, an opportunity I felt I had been deprived of so far. But whatever the scenario or the thought it was always fuelled by one thing, anger.

This with this boiled over however, when one day I got into an argument with a random lad on Facebook over something stupid. I felt like I was justified in making him pay for some imaginary wrongdoing so using Facebook I found out who his wife was, and I sent her a message telling her that I had seen him kissing another woman in a bar on Christmas eve. It was total bullshit, a complete fabrication to try and cause him problems in his relationship and to this day one of the biggest dick moves I've ever made. To this day I still regret doing this and what bugs me more is I was proud that I had gone this far in my imaginary crusade for justice. This quickly came back to bite me in the arse though when Kels phone rang first thing the next morning. By this point Kel had decided to move away from counselling and began her own dog walking business which meant that her phone number was on the website, without much difficulty he'd found this and decided to tell her what I'd done. Kel confronted me, having not learnt my lesson from the last time and feeling embarrassed, I tried to bullshit my way out of it but fairly quickly the truth came out. I felt like a piece of shit (because I was one) and hated the person I had become. I knew that I had to do something to try and make it right. I got in touch with him and apologised, I couldn't justify why I'd done what I had (because there is no justification for that) so I just told him I was mentally fucked and needed help. I don't know if he believed me or not, but he was a proper gent about it and accepted my apology. What made what I'd done feel so much worse was that I found out that he was a veteran. Knowing what forces couples go through and how much infidelity goes on behind the wire I couldn't believe I'd just tried to break him up with his wife. I still speak to him every now and then, we're both into target shooting so we chat about that but every time we talk, I feel a compulsion to apologise for being a colossal bellend.

Things got worse a few days later. One day during work I had gone home to walk Meg, while driving back to camp I showed my pass at the gate and drove on, as usual I was in a complete daze, the fuzziness had taken over and I was coasting through life, staring into the nothingness. Like those 2 times just after I got back from my tour but now it was a permanent state. As I drove further onto camp a group of Saudi trainees were walking along the path. These guys were a common sight on camp, they had been sent there by the Saudi military to be instructed in aircraft maintenance. Other than passing them out and about it was rare we crossed paths but what experience I did have with these guys it usually wasn't good. Many of them were arrogant, cocky, dossing about like everyone else was beneath them. They had no respect for anyone else, so I had no respect for them, a few times I'd found myself berating one of them after pushing in at a queue or showing a lack of respect to someone, usually a woman. It wasn't my place to do this, I was a lesser rank than many of them but the rank system meant nothing to them when they spoke to our lot so it meant nothing to me, also I doubt they understood most of what I was saying. Also, as I was now a fully-fledged arsehole, rank meant little to nothing to me even at the best of times (looking back, I think my attitude stank as much as theirs, I just hid behind the excuse of being mental). But on this occasion when these lads were walking down my path, they weren't Saudi trainee's, they were military aged middle eastern males and as such they posed a likely threat to everyone's safety. As I drove, they turned towards the road and started crossing without looking, this meant that they were now crossing my path. This was fairly common as they had an attitude of 'you will wait for me'. One of them at the back of the group was taking his time, he looked directly at me and looked away, expecting me to slow for them. Except I didn't, in my mind these guys were potential terrorists. They were Middle Eastern, in military fatigues, and acting like arseholes. In my mind this was evidence enough that someone was up to no good and something had to be done (I never said I was any good at profiling, I just said I did it a lot!). I started to speed up, driving a little 1.2 litre Fiesta meant that it made enough noise for them to take notice, realising that no matter how cock sure you are, a 1 tonne metal missile was going to win this battle, the straggler at the back sped up towards the other side. But I couldn't let him escape, this guy was a terrorist suspect! This was my chance to make that difference I had been wanting to make. So, I continued to speed up and began turning into the other side of the road, towards where he now was. He ran to the curb and got there safely with inches to spare, not wanting to plough the car into a tree I swerved back onto my side of the road and slowed down.

For the last minute of the journey I thought nothing of this, until I pulled into a parking space and turned my engine off. Then it hit me, I'd just tried to run this guy over, and he wasn't a terrorist, he was a Saudi soldier. And whilst he was still an arrogant arsehole, he was innocent of whatever I assumed he had done or was about to do. In the space of 60 seconds I'd graduated from fully fledged arsehole to a danger to others. For years I wondered if medically I could be classed as a danger to others, I figured that if I was, I would be locked away somewhere but wondered how bad things would have to get for this to happen. But now there was no question about it, my mind had decided that an innocent bloke was a terrorist and therefore I'd tried to kill him. Looking back, I don't think my heart was in it, if it was, I would have driven faster and been willing to mount the foot path. But I didn't want to hurt him and would have been devastated if I had of succeeded in my one-man mission of imaginary counter terrorism. It was more a case of 'Well I'm here, I'll take this guy out and then get myself to work. As if I was multi-tasking by combining my daily commute to work with casual murder, as you do.

After this I knew something had to change, and now. I'd become someone that I hated, my missus was seeing a side of me she never wanted to see, I wasn't even a man anymore, a man doesn't do shit like that. I was a shell of a person. My functions in life had been stripped back to basics, eating, sleeping and shitting. Even getting showered and dressed was a no go some days. I couldn't wait 6 weeks and Kel knew this. Without me knowing she went to the med centre and spoke to another doctor. She told me how worried she was about me and that I needed help now. The doc listened to her and agreed to see me, I went back to the med centre and made sure that I saw the same doctor that she has spoken to. This doctor was different, a young military lad, friendly and seemed eager to help. Rather than the last bloke who was a senior officer, looked like he was nearing retirement and stopped giving a shit several years back. I told him that I was at rock bottom and knew I needed help now or I couldn't go on anymore, I had no control of my own thoughts or feelings and felt like I was at risk of not being on control of my own actions. I then did something that I had never done before, even after all my appointments with the various medical professionals, I had never looked any of them in the eye and said 'I need help'. Although it was clear from the get-go that I needed help I'd always skirted around saying it for fear of showing too much weakness in front of someone. Even then I wanted to keep my military man persona up, even during the times when I cried, I tried to make it clear that I was crying because I had no other option to, as if anyone would, no matter how tough or hard-nosed they were. But this time it felt different, my wall which I had put up to stop anyone getting too close was down, my ego was non-existent, and I didn't have the energy to put up a façade anymore. Saying these three words felt like a last-ditch attempt to get help. At the time I wondered if my façade had prevented the docs from seeing what was really going. I don't see how psych professionals could fail to see what was going on beneath the surface, but it crossed my mind that maybe I'd been the cause of this whole lack of effective treatment all this time.

Leaving the doctors that time was a world away from the times before, I felt like he'd really listened to me. He called my shrink while I was still sat there and asked to get me an urgent appointment as he was concerned for my safety. Normally hearing someone say they were concerned for my safety due to my mental health would have made me shit myself, it's not something you hear every day and usually means that the shit has well and truly hit the fan. But I knew this already, there was no denying that things were seriously fucked up and that I was a danger to myself and others. As my appointment with this doc came to an end, he gave me one piece of advice which will stick with me for the rest of my life. He looked me in the eye and said "I know it feels bad right now, but whatever you're going through it will get better". The fact that he actually seemed to give a shit about me and was willing to show this compassion took me back. I didn't show it or say anything at the time, but this one simple bit of advice would stay with me and would help pull me through.

I was given an appointment to see my shrink the next day, I made the same journey I'd made loads of times by this point. Every journey before it had felt like a wasted journey because I'd come away from it feeling like we'd failed to tackle the root cause. Maybe this time it would be different. I got to DCMH, a small, single story brick building with a plain beige interior, it always bugged me that a building dedicated to the recovery of psychological issues of people in the forces had the same look and feel as every other building in the military. I felt as though it should be somewhere where a person could escape the monotony and protocol of military life. On this occasion I noticed a slight change, they'd went out and bought a rug for the reception, a large fish tank and some cacti for the waiting area. I laughed to myself because the walls were still beige, people were still dossing about in military rig and they still had photos of military shit on the walls. Including a photo of a chinook helicopter kicking up the sand and dust in somewhere hot and sandy, troops running off the ramp at the back, I thought this was a stupid idea because chances are some of the guys in there would associate an image like this with a shitty time in their past.

After a short wait, I was called through to see the doc, I sat down and told him everything that had gone on. I remember sitting there, feeling weak, both mentally and physically but also as a man, I was broken and wanted him to know it. I didn't care how weak I looked, I just wanted to get this sorted. I don't remember what was said specifically in that session, all I do remember is the doc was non-committal in what he was saying, no diagnosis, no plan of action, no encouraging words, just the usual meaningless dross. I asked him to treat me, to give me something that would help but he told me that because I was so ill and fragile that it was the wrong time to proceed with any therapy. I would need to be in a better place before they begun therapy. He increased my medication and sent me on my way. I asked him again to give me some kind of test for PTSD but he refused, saying that my PTSD symptoms were knock on effects of my chronic depression and side effects of my medication. I was crushed, what was it going to take before they would act and get me sorted? Would I need to kill someone, or myself?

I'd changed beyond any recognition as a person, I'd lost my identity, my compassion, I was trying to break up happily married couples, I was trying to dish up my own lethal justice on imaginary enemies and my temper was getting the better of me at work, swinging my fists around where they weren't welcome and unleashing tirades of abuse at whoever, or whatever happens to be in front of me at the time.

I'd fallen as far as I could fall, I couldn't get any lower I hated myself, I hated everyone around me, I hated life and felt like I wasn't just at the bottom of the barrel, I was managing to dig deeper down to depths I didn't know existed. But I was still here, it hadn't beaten me yet, which meant there must have been something of me left somewhere in there, the only way I could go now was up.

Chapter 18

The precipice

SAC White must not talk like a WW2 era pilot on the radio

The next few months followed in the same bullshit way. Brief, pointless sessions at DCMH. Most of my sessions consisted of another mental test resulting in the same worryingly high scores followed by a 15-minute chat that would lead to the session ending with me struggling to find some kind of benefit of me having gone there. I don't remember much from this time. I was in such a dark and lonely place in my mind that I think it's shut off that entire period of my life. I couldn't tell you anything that happened in those months. From talking to Kel the only thing I do know is I was now having more night terrors than ever. Wildly punching, kicking and thrashing about in bed, screaming about not being able to help people I was watching die. On a couple of occasions, I'd either wake myself up or Kel would wake me up and in an instant, I'd start crying into my pillow, Kel couldn't settle me, she just held me until I calmed down (Shit the bed, this part is harder to write than I thought!). For the most part I was still in work at this point but had brief periods of being off work when I just couldn't bring myself to leave the house. I would sit on the sofa, hoodie over my head, no idea what was going on around me. I'd sit and feel completely empty, miserable, the dark clouds consumed my mind, the storm blowing the shards of my

131

brain around, so I couldn't make sense of my own thoughts. Anytime there was a brief respite I was brought crashing back down again by something that put me back into that zone in my mind. At the time, ISIS were in full flow and attacks on civilians were a weekly occurrence, every time there was an attack it sent me off on my usual pattern of anger, then pouring over the details of what happened, which would make me angrier. Then I'd start feeling low again and back at square one. It felt relentless and a few times I considered ending it all. I thought about how I would do it. I could drive my car into a wall or a lamp post, maybe I could grab a knife and charge at the gate guard, forcing them to do it for me. I thought about ways I could make it look like I'd tried so the shrink would take me seriously, I could hurt myself badly but not so badly that I'd kill myself. I wasn't bothered about my life, my life didn't mean anything to me, I was a shell of a person anyway so why would it? The only thing that kept me going was Kel and Meg, I couldn't do it to them. I knew how much Kel loved me. I felt a responsibility to meg to stick around, protect her and give her a good life. Sometimes I felt like they would be better without me as a burden, when this happened all I had was what that doctor said to me "whatever you're going through it will get better". I kept telling myself that nothing lasts forever, I reminded myself of times in my life when I felt like a tough time would never end but eventually it did. I made a conscious decision to tattoo this inside my brain; "nothing lasts forever, it will end".

Things have gotten pretty dark again, haven't they? I did warn you. Let's take a break again with another story from the book of 'stupid shit that's happened to me'.

Back in 2013 I went on to Prague for my stag do with a group of mates. It was your typical kind of arrangement, 3 days consisting of shit loads of booze, time on a shooting range, strippers and more booze. I even stole the hat off a bloke who I'm pretty sure was a Mafioso. On our last night we were all hanging out from a diet of takeaway, lager and sleep deprivation, we decided to have one last big night with what little money we had left. So, we went out into town to find cheap booze and cheap strippers (not that there is such a thing). After beers in several bars we found a strip club where the ladies danced on the bar so we could get a dance by just paying for the drinks. This place was dodgy as fuck. Strip joints aren't known for being luxurious places but this place was next level seedy and ran by gangsters who looked like they wouldn't hesitate at taking you out the back of the club to feed you your own feet.

After an hour of us buying only one drink each and not giving the girls on the bar any money for their skills, the staff were getting annoyed at us obviously taking the piss. The girls began demanding money off each of us or we'd have to leave. Clive (as he'll be known in this book), one of the lads with us was a top, bloke, funny as fuck but a walking hand grenade after several drinks. He started searching his pockets for cash to give the girl in front of him. Unable to find any decent money he started counting change out on the bar while the stripper looked on wondering what the fuck he was doing. With the girl knelt down in front of him, legs splayed out behind her with not a piece of material on her apart from some high heels, Clive tried to hand the coins over to her; obviously insulted by this pathetic gesture she shunned the change and told him to piss off in Czech. Frustrated that his 'generous' gesture wasn't appreciated he picked up the change and threw it directly at her lady parts. Without missing a beat, I grabbed Clive by the arm and ushered the rest of the lads out the club knowing that we were in for a kicking if we didn't scarper. We spent the rest of the night asking each other 'Penny for your vagina?'.

As I write this it's occurred to me that the last 3 random stories, I've told have all painted me in a less than favourable light when it comes to the fairer sex. Just to clear up any worries, I was young, dumb and usually drunk and as with many others, most of the stupid shit I did when I was younger involved ladies because I was fucking clueless when it comes to them (I suspect I still am). These stores in no way reflect the respect I hold for our ovarian counterparts, I practically worship the ground my wife walks on and show just as much respect to lasses as I do to blokes. Just thought I'd clear that up as I don't want any angry emails or phone calls.

Anyway, back to the book.

Looking back at how I was feeling back then, hopeless, lost, worthless and suicidal. I think this was the tipping point, I could either continue to wait for something to happen, receive no support and end up doing something

I would regret, or I could take ownership of my situation start trying to improve things. Because DMCH were failing to do anything useful and there was no sign of them doing anything soon. I decided to take things into my own hands. I found myself a private counsellor called Michelle Johnson, who was not far away from me. At the start, I had no idea if this would be a good move or not, but I was sick of waiting and at this point would do anything to get my shit together, even a little. I decided to be open with the military shrink about wanting to see a private therapist as bullshitting had bitten me in the arse in the past. The reaction was frosty, the MOD weren't keen on me seeing anybody about my issues except them, they said it was in case they somehow cocked it up and made me worse this felt like a shite reason to me because I certainly wasn't getting any better. It took several meetings and phone calls before anyone agreed, they made me sign a waiver form to say that if I chose to do this it was under my own steam, they're not responsible for anything that happens as a consequence and that it wasn't recommended by them. Knowing that in 5 years I had achieved nothing with DCMH, I gladly signed it.

I was firmly shitting myself about my first session with Michelle, I knew that I would have to explain everything again. I also knew that my story wasn't what anyone would consider a 'typical' one and I fully expected to be asked if I was going to kill myself like the 32 times before. No really, I was asked this over 32 times, I'm convinced that this contributed to my suicidal thoughts, it's like if you asked someone 32 times if they wanted to rob a bank. Initially they would say no, but eventually they're going to start thinking if they should rob a bank. I was worried I'd get the same non-committal answers from Michelle that I'd gotten so far, I also expected intrusive questions about my childhood but none of this was worth not giving this a go, I had to. I was also looking forward to it, I could get an opinion of a professional from outside the military, who, by now I suspected were reluctant to diagnose PTSD because I didn't fit the mould of what they expected PTSD to look like or because a PTSD diagnosis would be an admission of guilt on their part because nothing else was going to cause this other than my work in Afghan, and that could get expensive for them.

Instantly, speaking with Michelle felt different to every other session with the psych staff at DCMH, it felt like she was actually listening to what I was saying. She asked minimal questions, and those she did ask were only to get a better understanding of what was going on. We briefly spoke about my childhood but then quickly moved back to my time in the military. Although I was talking about stuff that I found tough I found it easy to speak to her. To me, this felt like a well-rehearsed story because I'd had to go over it so many times by now, with the mental health nurses, the shrinks, the docs in the med centre and my chain of command back on Leeming. It had become a script I could reel off to anyone without it bothering me but this time I felt like telling her everything would actually have a positive outcome. Even the room she used for her therapy sessions felt different, no beige or stupid pictures of military shit. It felt like a home, warm, comfortable, somewhere that you didn't mind spilling your guts, even to a complete stranger.

I don't remember much of these sessions; my brain was basically mush and I feel like that in order to protect me from having to deal with all that shit again it, my head has said 'yeah let's just put that away in this little dark corner, shall we?' which in all honesty, I'm fine with, I'm more interested in looking forward to my future than remembering the shitty details of my past. What I do remember is feeling like we were actually doing therapy. We spoke about different ways of thinking about what had happened, what I was getting from all this anger and why I felt like what was bothering me, bothered me in relation to my values and what's important to me, after the 3rd session she even confirmed that she believed I as suffering from depression and PTSD. This felt like a major vindication and although I knew the military shrinks would never listen to her, I trusted her professional opinion much more than theirs. After each session I walked out feeling lighter, like a little weight had been lifted off my shoulder and a bit more reassured that somehow, I could crack this.

After a few weeks seeing Michelle I was a long way from sorting out my issues, but she had given me hope that there were people out there who could and would help me. One morning all this came crashing down in an instant when I got a call from my military pysch doc. He asked me to come in and see him that afternoon, he'd already spoken to my management and told them, so I was to report to him without going anywhere else, including into work. This was the first time that anybody in the military side of psych care had actually grown some balls and taken some kind of initiative, so although I was confused by this new development, I was kind of excited as well. Doing as I was told I waited out at home until the time for my appointment came and I drove over to see the doc.

The minute I walked in the office something was different, the doc looked like he'd just lost a winning lottery ticket, no smiles, no welcome, just 'come in and sit down'. Here's how the conversation went:

Doc "*Pete, I had a call from the RAF Police…*"

Me "*Wankers*"

Doc "*….Yes, well. They told me something which has concerned me and they're concerned for your safety. They have had a report that you have been watching videos of people being beheaded*"

Me "*What the fuck? That's bullshit doc, they're lying little bastards!*"

Doc "*Are you sure? Because someone has reported this to the police*"

I don't remember much of the rest of this conversation; I just remember that I went ape shit. The fact of the matter was that this was bullshit, I had seen some fucked-up stuff on videos of insurgents getting hit but I hadn't been watching videos of people being deprived of their noggin. This is exactly what I told the doc, I'd told him before that I'd been watching these videos but when

I said it this time, he looked surprised and denied that I'd ever told him this.

I hit boiling point, I'd spent years asking these guys for help and they failed to do anything, the only time they were proactive is when they wanted to accuse me of something I hadn't done and now they had just proved they weren't listening to what I said in the first place. The doc was curious and asked me why I watched the videos,

Me *"They're vermin, rats, a cancer that need cutting out and if I don't get the fucking chance to do to myself then I'll enjoy watching others get the opportunity"*

Doc *"What do you mean do it yourself?"*

I told him about my half-baked plan to fly over there, grab a gun and turn into some kind of low budget Rambo. I told him how I'd been looking up flights, researching where I could go, what I'd do when I got there, maybe join the Peshmerga in Syria, kill as many of the bad guys as I could before my time came. This was the first time I had told anyone of this and looking back this was probably a good thing, because (as we established earlier) it was a completely mental idea, but in my mind, at the time this was a perfectly reasonable idea. By this point it was clear that the Doc was finally paying attention to me because he was obviously concerned. *"Why do you want to do that Pete?"* he said, *"Because they deserve to die and so far, I've done fuck all to help"* I replied, my voice gradually getting louder as I went on.

Doc *"But you're an engineer Pete, it's not your job to kill people"*

Me *"So?"*

Doc *"So you would be doing this as a civilian, not a member of the military because it's not your job"*

Me *"I don't give a shit!"*

Doc *"But Pete, that's murder, you would be murdering people"*

Me *"No because they're not fucking people! I told you, they're vermin! How can I be a murderer when they're not people!? And let's face it, they've never been worried about murdering innocent people so why are you worried about someone killing them!?"*

I realised I was stood up, shouting at the doc, seething with rage, spitting as I spoke. I remember seeing the worry in his eyes, it crossed my mind that he might hit the attack alarm he had on his desk. To meet me at my level the Doc stood up too but kept his voice low and calm. He encouraged me to apply reason and logic to my plan, gradually breaking it down into a step-by-step process so I could see how ridiculous it actually was. This went on for about 15 minutes until he managed to talk me down. Initially I accepted it would be murder, but I didn't care, then I accepted that it was a stupid plan, but I didn't care, eventually accepting that I the whole thing was dumb as fuck and would never happen.

Once I'd calmed down and started to see some sense the doc started to ask about my meds. He wanted to check that I was still taking venlafaxine, that I was taking it properly and I wasn't on anything else. After some in-depth questioning, he came to the conclusion that I was having some kind of reaction to it and was sending me off the rails. He told me to get myself off those meds in 2 weeks, which is at least 3 months quicker than they would recommend anyone do normally. He also prescribed me a drug called Olanzapine, he just said it was to settle me down and to help with the anger, but not much else. To save you a boring google search, it turns out it's an anti-psychotic drug. Further down the line I found out that I'd had a major reaction to the Venlafaxine the second time I'd been prescribed it, it sent me head off on its own little journey of crazy and I ended up having mini psychotic episodes which were forcing me to lose tough with reality. When they told me this I thought back to when I was younger, watching movies and thinking that it would be fun being a psycho because you could do whatever you want and nobody could stop you, completely free of all responsibility or accountability. In reality, its shit, scary as fuck and nothing about it is fun oh, and you're still held accountable for your actions, so you can't hit people and have people just shrug their shoulders and say 'well he's crazy so it's ok'. Trust me, I asked, a lot.

The news that I had been having psychotic episodes brought on mixed feelings, it was partly a relief because I had a reason why I was so off the rails recently and maybe now I had a chance of them actually doing something to fix me. On the other hand, it scared the shit out of me because I didn't know what to expect or what was going to happen, and I wasn't sure what was real and what was my own little imaginary world of crazy. Would I end up locked up for my own good or being monitored somehow? I also had to take a crash course on what it meant to have a psychotic episode because in my head it was some kind of Texas chainsaw massacre type stuff. Turns out psychotic is a term for someone who is losing touch with reality, but they can still be a good person and want to do good. Like in my case I wanted to do good by ridding the world of terrorists, but the psychotic part comes in when I thought that I could travel over there, somehow find a rifle and magically develop Hollywood special forces type skills to kill a load of bad guys. It's different to a psychopath, this is a personality disorder which describes someone who lacks any kind of empathy, moral compass, is prone to lying to get what they want and is generally a total arsehole. A psychopath is also usually a constant way of life for someone, because it's their personality. Whereas a psychotic person will usually have episodes where they drift in and out of it. A psychopath who is having psychotic episodes are usually the guys you see on the news after they've done something horrendous but thankfully, that's pretty rare.

While speaking about getting enjoyment from watching the videos of the bad guys getting hit the doc asked me to describe what I got from it. I told him I got a kick out of it, it was a release, made me laugh. He then asked me how I felt after watching it; I'd never really thought about this, but I always felt shit after watching it and a few days after I'd always feel crap. He told me the videos were a form of self-harm, I had tried the whole cutting myself thing, I'd tried drinking, making myself throw up, at one point I even tried hitting myself but none of it worked for me. In watching these videos I'd found something that worked, it felt like a type of justice and because I'd largely been completely useless during my tour, somehow it made me feel like I was part of it. I sometimes wonder if I would have been better off joining a different service or a more combat oriented trade. That may have helped me feel more useful but realistically, it began to dawn on me that I was never cut out for that stuff. Loads of people want to be a soldier and kill the bad guy, until it comes time to do soldier stuff and they see what's really involved. The reality is I haven't got the right mind-set for that kind of role and as much as I wanted to be some kind of elite special forces operator, I wasn't, and I would never be. I was Pete, a computer geek in the Royal Air Force and aside from that, my mind and body wasn't built for that kind of stuff. This made the docs next request pretty easy to accept, he asked me to stop watching the videos completely. A concept which I found a little difficult to stomach because I'd always associated them with that release and I'd grown addicted to them, but now, I could see what they were actually doing and how I was trying to be something I'm not; I was prepared to do it. It felt like giving up a full-blown addiction and afterwards I did find some-times where something would make me want to do it again, to get that release, the same kind of release someone gets from cutting themselves but to this day I haven't don't it again. Looking back now it feels like something really minor and stupid but back then felt like a real challenge, but it was the first major step in my recovery.

Chapter 19

Clawing my way back

SAC White must not complete a sex change form and submit it to admin

6 years ago, I'd never given mental health a second thought. I thought being depressed meant you were sad, being psychotic meant you were a dangerous, crazy criminal. Anxiety meant you were scared of something and I had never even heard of PTSD. Now, I was suicidal, having real psychotic episodes which meant I had tried to run a random bloke over in my car, I was permanently anxious about terrorist attacks to the extent where I once took a knife with me to a friend's wedding because it was a wealthy family automatically meant that in my head that it was a target for some kind of attack or robbery and I needed to protect people (and this seemed perfectly reasonable to me at the time) and was crippled by the multitude of symptoms brought on by PTSD. I was a mess and I had nearly given up hope of ever getting better. Despite my best efforts, my positive affirmations of 'Things will get better' and 'Nothing lasts forever' weren't achieving jack shit and things just appeared to be getting worse. I had been let down by the management in Afghan who gave me a non-existent job that left me fucked up. I felt like I had been betrayed by my chain of command in Leeming, who treated me like some kind of outcast before kicking me when I was down, and I felt like I'd just been betrayed by the very

people here to help and protect me when my doc and the RAF police accused me of something I hadn't done. Not only that but it looked like the report to the RAF Police, had come from someone within my own workplace; the same lads I spoke to openly about my issues and trusted to at least provide a sympathetic ear.

After the session with the psych doc where everything came bursting out, he'd finally clocked what was going on and seemed to realise that something needed to be done. He changed the tune he'd been playing for the last 6 or 7 months of 'Let's wait for things to get a bit better' and began singing a different tune, one more along the lines of 'Holy shit, let's get this sorted'. We began talking more in depth about where this all started, when I first noticed things going wrong and how I felt about it all now. Our time together felt much more like proper therapy sessions, rather than the 20 minute "*How are you feeling?*", "*Shit*", "*OK see you next week*" sessions I'd grown accustomed to.

After a couple of sessions of talking like this, he finally diagnosed me with PTSD. This didn't exactly come as a shock to me, I had been under no doubt for months that I had PTSD but meant that I could finally start getting the correct treatment. I still believed that what I had was in fact CPTSD, but I was prepared to take whatever victories I could, providing it means I got treatment. He told me that he was going to arrange for me to have some trauma therapy, followed by Cognitive Behavioural Therapy (CBT), and some anger management sessions.

The trauma therapy was Eye Movement Desensitization and Reprocessing or EMDR for short. This is a widely used treatment for sufferers with PTSD.

EMDR treatment is built around the idea of how we process events in our lives while we sleep. When we're in deep sleep and dreaming our eyes dart left to right, during this our mind processes events over the day, week, month or even years before. Normally we have no idea that this is happening, EMDR replicates this but with the person awake. I did my treatment with a lady known only as Liz (not because her identity is secret, because that's all I ever knew her as). I took a while to warm to Liz, partially because she was a MOD therapist and had to work to the same protocols and framework as the rest of them but also because by this point, I didn't want to have to open up to someone else only to be shot down again. The first couple of sessions I kept my guard up and we talked about surface level stuff, not wanting to give too much away and protect myself from being hurt. After a while I began to feel comfortable with her and began to open up a bit more. She told me about EMDR, what it was, why they used it and how it could help. Being someone who prefers tangible tools and techniques to tackle problems rather than woo-woo therapies where feelings and emotions are discussed, I was keen to give this a go.

Things started off with a couple of sessions of talking over every aspect of my time in Afghan, from start to finish, from the major events to the minor details in as much detail as I could remember. As I spoke, she wrote things down and ended up with a few pages of what I'd said. She told me that in our EMDR we would talk about the events that I had found upsetting or troubling, drag them up from the corners of my mind and reprocess them in a way that was more helpful. She also asked me to think of a safe place I could go to in my mind if things got too much while we did the therapy. It had to be somewhere I've actually been, ideally nobody else would be there and I found it relaxing and peaceful. They used this as a kind of safety net if things got too intense during the therapy or the session time was nearly up, but you were in the middle of processing something difficult, they would tell you to go to your safe place until things settled down a bit. I opted for the canal 15 minutes from my house. I'd taken Meg there one day during the summer. I loved this place; the water was clear enough to see the fish and the bottom of the canal, the sun poked through the trees causing the water to glisten. Everyone was at work so nobody was about and the only noise you could hear was the birds and the trees rustling in the breeze. I sat on the side of the bank with meg for half an hour and just chilled out. This is easier said than done when you have a Border Collie who just wants to be on the move all the time but it's one of my favourite places and somewhere easily accessible to me.

Old school EMDR usually consisted of someone holding a pen in front of your face and moving it side to side, your eyes following it. Thankfully, things had moved on a bit and they had technology to help with this. The most common was a long, flat row of lights, the light would move side to side like Kitt from Knight

Rider. Personally, I opted for 2 small vibrating balls which reminded me of sex toys. You would hold one in each hand and they would vibrate quickly changing back and forth. I preferred this because it meant that I could close my eyes and picture what I was talking about as I'm a pretty visual person. After a few sessions preparing for the therapy, the day came. It was a grey, overcast and wet day, I was nervous about the EMDR therapy because I wasn't sure if it would help me, have no effect or even make me worse by having to go through everything again in more detail than I'd ever done before. But I was also excited to start getting some traction on my treatment and start working towards some form of recovery.

I can't tell you if this is the same for everyone but here's how my EMDR played out.

1.   The therapist gets you nice and chilled out using breathing exercises
2.   They'll show you how the buzzers (or lights) work so you've got an idea of what to expect
3.   They'll ask you to talk about one of the times which you've found difficult. This is where Liz used her notes to prompt me when I had trouble recalling
4.   After a minute or so of speaking about the event you'll stop, and they'll start the buzzers or lights alternate side to side while you process what you were just talking about

5.   The therapist will ask you to take a snapshot of the event in your mind, usually a key moment in what happened, then more side to side stuff

6.   The therapist will then ask you to either shrink this snapshot down a bit, or turn it black and white or manipulate the image in some way, more side to side stuff

7.   They'll repeat this again and again until the image is tiny, black and white and maybe out of focus.

I spoke about getting the reports in about the guys being hit, seeing the videos and pictures of these events. I spoke about the dead, burnt child, even some of the videos I'd watched under my own steam when I got home. One by one I turned each event snapshot into a black and white, half a postage stamp-sized image. We followed the same process for each subject and as we worked through them, I gradually found myself giving less of a shit about each one. It's not that they weren't awful in their own right, what happened would always be crap, there's no changing that but by reprocessing each one they became less important to me. Each time we changed the size or the colour of the image it created the concept in my mind, then forcing my brain to act as if I was dreaming cemented the idea so it stuck. After my EMDR session I felt lighter, like a huge weight had been lifted off my shoulders. As I walked out of the DCMH building the entire world seemed brighter; I was sure the gloomy, overcast conditions were still the same as an hour ago, but it just seemed brighter. I sat in McDonalds for a while after (as per the tradition) and mulled things over. I felt exhausted; mentally and physically drained, in a haze but also relieved. Everything that we had discussed had still happened, and they were all still shit, but they felt less important to me now. It felt like breaking a leg, at the time it was really shite, after it hurt like a bastard and it held me back but with the proper treatment the break had healed, I was ready to start working on getting my life back again.

Most people need several EMDR sessions, some need them long term, I only needed one. I don't know what that meant, whether whatever had gone wrong in my head to cause the PTSD was easily fixable or maybe I just got lucky and took to the therapy really well. Either way I felt like I'd been freed from the shackles of PTSD and things were finally starting to improve. The next few days I was exhausted, I felt like I'd run a marathon and spent the majority of my time sleeping. It wasn't lost on me that what we'd done hadn't been a treatment for the depression and I still had a lot more work to do in that respect.

I see mental health as an overflowing sink. Normally life's troubles and shitty times spend a brief amount of time in the sink and then flow down the plug hole. With mental health something has blocked the plug, meaning that everything else that happens can't flow away, it just builds up until it eventually over flows. Without someone stepping in to help you clear the blockage it'll always be there. Of course, you can take steps to bail some of the water (shittyness) out with medication, finding something you enjoy and helps you forget about what's going on, and things will temporarily ease up again but eventually, it's going to fill up again because what's causing the blockage is still there. For me, what had happened in Afghan had caused a blockage which had gone unnoticed for years. The docs had agreed that there was a blockage but wouldn't agree what was causing it. To keep up with the plumbing analogy (let's see how far I can drag this out) The military psych guys had been trying to clear it with tweezers when it needed some industrial stuff. When they had finally pulled their fingers out of their arses and treated the right condition with the right tools, things had improved.

Something else which wasn't lost on me was the fate of my career in the RAF, I was well aware that things were too far gone for me to ever have a decent career, my chance of promotion was somewhere between 'Never gonna happen' and 'not a fucking chance'. My name would always be tarnished as 'the mental one'. An association that wasn't helped a few months prior to my EMDR treatment when an accident with an airgun resulted in me looking like I'd shot myself in the head.

See, one of my escapes from everything that been going on was target shooting. I loved that it helped me clear my head of everything. Getting the shot on target, the sense of achievement when I got the shot I was after and the lack of people around me while I was doing it. Another aspect I enjoyed was how the guns could be customised to suit the shooter. I had bought a second hand, cheap Chinese gun from a lad on Facebook (mistake #1) who had already done a lot of work on customising it. I then went about changing various parts of the gun myself using stuff I'd read about online (mistake #2). Typically, once I'd got it to a point where I was happy with it, I decided to sell it on for something better. I found a buyer and before packaging it up to be sent to its new owner, I decided to change one last part of the gun. A 1 inch in diameter gas plug which screwed on the end of the gas barrel which created a seal for the 2 CO_2 canisters inside. I dry fired the gun for a while until it hissed with gas, a clear sign that it was empty and no longer had pressure to hold the seals in place, resulting in the remaining gas escaping in a long hiss. Confident that it was empty I tried unscrewing the gas plug at the end, but it wouldn't budge. This either meant that it was still under pressure or was cross threaded. Confident that it wasn't under pressure I grabbed a wrench and went to town on it. With the butt off the rifle on the floor and the gas barrel facing my head as I looked down on it (massive mistake #3) I gradually unscrewed the gas plug. Then with the loudest bang I've ever heard the gas plug exploded from the gun, straight into my forehead. This was closely followed by one of the CO_2 canisters. Leaving the gun at a rate of knots, they glanced off my head, shooting into the ceiling plaster work of my house, hitting a wooden joist, bouncing back down through the ceiling and settled on the carpet. The Mrs and the dog were shitting themselves in equal measure, somehow it didn't knock me out and I knew instantly what had happened; seeing the blood now pissing down onto the carpet and the gun below and suspecting that I now had a gaping hole in my head, I grabbed a towel, telling Kel to call 999. A few minutes later, after throwing up in the toilet from the shock, I suspected I'd pass out soon, so I put myself in the recovery position by the front door, hopefully making it easy for the paramedics to scoop me up and get me away. Eventually the front door opened, seeing a pair of black assault boots I expected to look up to see the orderly sergeant (A sergeant who was on duty out of normal working hours and deal with any incidents on camp) but instead seeing a Glock on this guys hip I realised it was the armed police. I hadn't realised it at the time but in her panic Kel had told the 999 operator that I had shot myself, so the police expecting to find a live gun in the house sent their armed response over. Seemingly not appreciating my greeting of 'oh shit, it's the fuzz!' he stepped over me, went through to check the airgun, seeing that it was a completely innocent (and stupid) situation, he returned a minute later, stepping over me again and walked out seemingly pissed off at the waste of his time.

The paramedics started patching me up and prepping me for a trip to A&E. Suddenly, I felt the most relaxed I had ever felt, with a blissful sense of calm and quiet. It turns out that I'd passed out. I wasn't impressed when the paramedic woke me up from my amazing sleep. In the ambulance I told the paramedics I was in loads of pain (I wasn't, I just really wanted the gas and air). Loving life on the gas & air and trying my best to look down the fit paramedic lasses top (Don't waste your time lads, they all wear high neck T-shirts) while Kel sat there rolling her eyes I started telling the paramedic all about watching people die in Afghan. Pissing myself laughing while describing how the insurgents arm flew in the opposite direction to his head when he was hit with a burst of 30 mm high explosive fire from an Apache. She sat there looking a little confused and horrified. All of a sudden, while crying with laughter talking about seeing some bad guys get blown up from a nose mounted camera on a missile I began uncontrollably crying, this transition barely distinguishable in the first few moments between laughter crying and normal crying. Turns out laughing gas & PTSD are a weird mix, who knew!?

Anyway, after getting stitched up by the docs and them telling me that they're amazed that I'm still alive given the size of the hole in my head they sent me on my way. What followed was days of gossip all over the base about the mental guy who tried and failed to shoot himself in the head, even had people telling Kel about it, not knowing that she was married to him.

Right, back to the story. Although the bulk of the blockage was now gone (the PTSD), some of it was still left over and needed sorting out (the depression). They tried to do this with CBT, which in a nut shell is the idea that how we think effects how we feel which dictates how we react and if we can change how we think and feel about certain things we can change how we think and feel we can change how we react. Initially, I found this difficult to accept, I mean how could I be responsible for my actions if the same chain of command who I trusted with my difficulties, accused me of faking everything to get out of work and who put me in a fake job for 10 weeks which fucked me up? Liz, kept at it, every time I found some bullshit argument as to why I wasn't responsible for my own actions she would quickly put me back in my place. She spoke about how else I could act if someone did that? Or how someone else might react? She helped me to see it from different perspectives.

During one session while we were talking about how I felt betrayed by people, how I didn't trust anyone and challenging my 'everyone is an arsehole' belief something just clicked. I interrupted Liz and said, "it doesn't matter, none of it matters". She stopped and looked at me quizzically, obviously trying to work out what I was on about. I felt like I'd had the sudden major breakthrough cliché you see in media where the person receiving therapy has a moment of enlightenment and suddenly understands what they need to do. I realised that for years these incidents with a few wankers had ruled every aspect of my life and by doing that it only brought me pain. I'd let these wankers dictate how I felt, how I acted, how I treat other people and myself. Yes, they were still wankers and they'd done me wrong but based on these few people I'd developed a mindset of 'Nobody can be trusted because they will fuck me over'. I had given them complete over my life. It made no sense. Apart from a few bad eggs, people are inherently good, the entire time I'd been ill, people were offering to help in whatever way they could, they'd listened to me piss and moan about every little thing. And even though these guys had done me wrong, it's possible that they may have been trying to do the right thing. Maybe they were trying to help me using the limited knowledge of mental health and my specific problems they had, and they were trying to help; just in a really, really stupid and naive way.

By this time, it had been decided by the powers that be in the MOD that I would be classified as 'non-effective' and my time in the forces was to come to an end on the 2nd July 2017. This decision didn't come as a shock to me, I'd decided months ago that the military and me weren't suited to each other and I made this crystal clear to whoever I spoke to. I hadn't been in to work for months after that period when things had gotten really dark and dangerous and I never would go back to work in the RAF. It was a shame that my planned long career had turned out like this but there was no way of knowing things would turn out this way when I joined back in 2009. If I had of just handed in my notice, I would have had to wait for 12 months before I could leave and would have left with nothing more than my last month's payslip. By getting a medical discharge it meant that I'd likely be out quicker, I would get a medical pension pay out and it would open certain doors to me to get specialised treatment and support with the NHS and forces charities should I ever need it.

After 6 sessions of CBT, Liz shook my hand and I left the DCMH building expecting to get call to book more sessions as we'd only just begun to scratch the surface of my depression. Although my EMDR had been super effective in 1 session, 6 years of severe depression wasn't going to get squared away in six 45-minute CBT sessions. Apart from one 5 minute chat with the Doc, that call never came, my treatment with DCMH had finished and I was on my own, effectively a civvy in all but name.

It was time to move on.

Chapter 20

Civvy Street

SAC White must not dry hump his Sergeant while he is on the phone, or at any other time for that matter.

With 6 months left in service my time in the military was all but over. Kel and I bought a house in a nice little market town in Shropshire and apart from a visit from a welfare Sergeant every few weeks I had nothing to do with the military. The visits from the welfare sergeant were always a pretty bland affair. She'd talk to me about what I was going to do for a job once the MOD released me to find a job, how I felt about the military in general and other menial bullshit. It was more a box ticking exercise than them actually giving a shit about my welfare and anything important rarely ever came out of these meetings. The real kicker came 3 weeks before my exit date, she asked me to hand in my military ID. I was never particularly attached to any of my military possessions, including my ID but all of a sudden, this little ID card which I'd taken for granted, meant so much to me. It gave me access to entire communities all over the country, for years it allowed me to get to my own house behind the base perimeter. We were only issued it once we passed basic and it felt like a membership to a very unique club. Even though I'd had a shit last few years in my service I didn't feel prepared to lose all of this. My career felt like it had suddenly ended without any kind of pomp and ceremony, thanks or recognition. I didn't really expect anything, but this signalled the actual end of my time in the forces and it consisted of me handing over a small white card to someone sat on my sofa. I hoped to hear someone from the guys on my last section at Cosford, maybe a phone call or a card but I got nothing. I haven't spoken to most of those guys since the day I last walked out of the office, not knowing at the time that it would be my last time.

I had never been the life and soul of the party during my time in the forces, but I had a few close mates who I got on well with. Lads I trusted and had stuck by me through everything. My ID card meant that although I was signed off work sick, I could get onto base and see them whenever I wanted. Suddenly, I'd lost this. I felt pretty lonely and started to doubt whether or not I could start all over again on civvy street.

3 months before my contract with the MOD came to an end, I got permission to find work in civvy street. I managed to land a job at an IT company who did IT support for companies all over the country. I had to blag my way through the interview because the Military have a habit of making you think that you're the mutts nuts at whatever job you did in the forces I thought I was the mutts nuts with computers. About 30 seconds into my interview I realised that by civilian standards, I knew fuck all. But the 'get shit done' mind-set and the confidence that the military instils in its personnel helped me to impress the managers interviewing me.

Researching every detail of the company (including their yearly turnover), and providing I had time to prepare some convincing sounding bullshit, I knew that I could blag with the best of them. The other thing that I think helped me was that I was honest about my health issues and that I was in the process of leaving the forces and getting into civvy street. This meant that I didn't have to bullshit about either of those things and it gave me permission to say 'I don't know' if they asked me a question about something which only civvys would understand.

Starting my first job in civvy street since I was pulling pints or stacking shelves in my younger years was pretty fucking scary. I was used to the brutal banter and the 'wind your neck in, stop moaning and just fucking do it!' approach to work in the military. Through years of being told so by the forces lads, I was convinced that the civilians would be jack bastards, unwilling to lift a finger to help anyone if it didn't benefit them personally. I worried that someone would rub me up the wrong way and I'd lose my shit with them; would I get in trouble for swearing? Did I have to call the boss Sir or ma'am? Would I get asked loads of stupid questions like 'Were you a pilot?' or 'have you ever killed anyone?' The minute I left my house on my first day I felt well and truly alone. I had no support network there, I couldn't exactly just pop home or go to the gym to get away if it wasn't going well, I didn't have any forces mates there. I had no fall back. It was up to me to make this work.

A week into my new job, it was painfully clear that I was well out of my depth. IT in the civilian world is a decade ahead of what's in place in the military and the little bits of information I did know were mostly out of date or considered bad practice. I started to doubt whether or not I could do this. Maybe I needed more time to transition, maybe I was jumping in too quick, maybe I was still too mentally ill to hold a job. I missed the military life, it was safe, predictable and I could tell people to piss off without getting fired. That's when I was offered the opportunity to attend a 'Battle Back' course ran by the Army, the Royal British Legion and Leeds University. Situated in the grounds of a beautiful manor house in the middle of woods in Shropshire; It's a course designed for troops who have been medically discharged for whatever reason; everything from a back injury from sport to limb loss caused from an IED blast to mental health issues. It's a week-long residential course run from the UK's centre for sporting excellence at Lilleshall in Shropshire. They use the same facilities as Olympic athletes and professional sportsmen and women. The idea of the course is to give folks who are going through a really shit time some confidence and motivation. Also, it was designed to help them to find a purpose when they're being forced to face with the idea of leaving the forces.

I jumped at the chance when I was offered a space on this course. I was missing life in the forces and the idea of spending some time with military bods who were in a similar position to me felt like exactly what I needed. I missed the mentality, the banter and the mindset.

Each day was a mix of loads of different activities, things like archery, climbing and even golf combined with lessons on self-discovery, development and confidence building. The first day of the course the whole lot of us got together to cover the basics and introduce ourselves. My intro consisted of something like "I'm Pete, I was a techy in the RAF, I've got PTSD from some shitty stuff in Afghan and I think everyone is an arsehole until they prove me wrong". No really, I said that to a room of 30+ military people I'd never met before. For all the progress I had made with my health, I still lacked any confidence, any self-respect or respect for other people and was still an arsehole. Thankfully people there understood what I meant, they got that I wasn't mentally all there and were willing to give me a chance, despite my introduction that made me look like a prize dick. I loved being around military personnel again, they understood how I spoke, if I told them about what had caused me to get fucked up, they got it without me needing to explain or justify anything. Up until this point I still felt like a fraud. Like if I told someone who came from the military world, they would think I was just making up shit for sympathy or attention. But nobody did, there was no judgement, people listened and understood. It was the first time I really felt validated. It also gave me the chance to hear their stories, what they had gone through and how mental health had affected them. Although the circumstances of what had happened to us were drastically different (some of these guys had been through unimaginable horrors), our symptoms, emotions and feelings were usually pretty similar. Other people spoke of the dark clouds, the constant anger, the same highs and lows. I learnt that I was far from alone, in fact, there are shit loads of guys and girls out there just like me. I learnt that if you open yourself up to communicating with people (both talking and listening) then you begin to learn that you're far from alone. You also learn that there are more than one way to solve a problem or tackle your issues. It broadens your horizons and opens doors you never even knew were there.

For all the moaning I've done about the military so far in this book; the Battle Back course and the guys running it are brilliant. The whole thing is designed to show you that you're capable of more than you think and after months or years of feeling completely useless the instructors have a way of building you back up. They helped us see that things could get better, and not only that but we had the power to improve our own lives. By the end of the week I had realised that if I thought that everyone else was an arse hole, chances are it was me being the arsehole and everybody just responded to me treating them like shit. Also, I not only felt like I could beat my issues with some work, but I felt like I could create a new me.

Although my health was much improved, I was still suffering from the effects of depression and knew that I needed to get myself squared away once and for all. The welfare sergeant suggested that I pick things up with the NHS. But waiting for several months only to start from scratch again with a completely new team of psych professionals to finish what the MOD should have finished in the first place really didn't appeal to me. I considered going back to speak to Michelle again, she had been a great help in my darkest period, and would no doubt be a great help at this point. I was close to giving her a call; but I had a lingering thought that I just couldn't shake. It was a thought that I had spent so long blaming other people for my position, and even more time relying on other people to get me out of that position. When I didn't have them, I just sat waiting for the next thing to happen to me, whether that be another terrorist attack to trigger my anxiety, some kind of bad news to trigger a depressive episode or someone doing something that would trigger my anger and I'd act like a dick. The whole thing had been years of me just letting life happen to me. Michelle was brilliant but I didn't want to rely on anyone else anymore, it was up to me.

Of course, there were aspects of my mental health which no doubt required professional intervention, certainly with my PTSD and the more serious aspects of my depression but here's the kicker (and some folk won't like this). I had chosen to be the victim the whole time. What had happened in the past was shit, but I had come to the realisation that I had chosen to stay in that chapter of my life and not move on. I blamed everyone else for the situation I was in and held on to that blame so intently that I couldn't move past it. Nobody could have ever told me this, I would have hit them. It took me to come to that realisation on my own before I could do anything about it.

I also seemed to identify as PTSD and depression rather than identify as Pete. When I met someone new, the 3rd or 4th sentence to leave my lips would be to tell them about my condition. But I was not depression, and I was not PTSD. Yes, I had those conditions, but they weren't me, I just suffered from the symptoms of those things, there's much more to me than that. But now that I had lost that identity of PTSD and was gradually losing the identity of depression what identity did I have? After all I'd lost most of my identity as a human and as a man during those dark times, I still couldn't feel emotion, I'd completely lost the old me, so what did I have? I felt like a painting that had been white washed, a blank canvas ready for me to create something new.

I decided that this is exactly what I would do. I had the opportunity to create a new me, and not in the 'new year, new me' bullshit sense. A completely fresh start with a fresh approach. The only problem is how would I get started? How do you build a new identity at the age of 30? Not knowing how to start I grabbed at the first thing that came to mind; YouTube. YouTube was full of self-development videos, many of them super corny and consisting mainly of American people shouting motivational stuff at you but it was a start. At the same time, I found an artist called 'Fearless Motivation' on a music streaming service, this was basically a collection of speeches by guys shouting motivational stuff at you and making pretty good cases for why you should get off your arse and get stuff done. Much the same as the YouTube videos they were great for a quick kick up the arse in the gym or on the way to work.

Both these tools I'd found discussed success, positive mindset, forming positive habits and overcoming adversity. All areas that I'd begun to get a real hunger for. It was a short-lived injection of motivation, but it was all I had to get me started and it lit a fire under my arse to push me to learn more. I became a bit (completely) interested in (obsessed with) the idea of success. What was success? How did successful people achieve their success? How could I replicate that? I started researching successful business people, inventors, celebrities, people who were at the top of their game. Not just minted (although having loads of cash would be nice), but people who had this whole life thing cracked. People who were happy, had great home lives, were experts in their fields, strived for growth and didn't let failure stop them. I figured if I learnt what successful people did and copied it then I could discover some form of success, even if it was a taste. I started looking into everything I could find to do with success, videos, songs, articles on the internet. It was all great, but it didn't feel like enough, it all felt like surface level stuff.

That's when I noticed a pattern in all this stuff I was looking at and listening to. Loads of it talked about the how successful people read loads and how powerful reading was. I had read about 3 books in my lifetime, one was the 'hungry hungry caterpillar', one was a Shakespeare book for my GCSE's and the other was Paul Gascoigne's autobiography when I was a teenager. I never had any interest in books and reading bored me to death. But if I wanted to copy what successful people did then all signs were pointing to books. Given that I didn't have the patience to sit down and read a book, I figured I could listen to audiobooks on my commute to my new job. But what should I read, or listen to? I didn't think Harry Potter would help me discover this new world of self-development that I was seeking, and I'd rather smash my head against a wall repeatedly then read about celebrities. Then suddenly I remembered that conversation with the physio back at RAF Cosford. He told me I should read a certain book, but what was it? That was years ago, and I can barely remember what happened last week, never mind when I had been up shit creek mentally.

Thankfully, at the time I thought it was a good enough idea to write it down on a note taking app on my phone. A habit which has since saved my arse more times than I can count. I even wrote the entire first chapter of this book on my phone. Seriously, if you don't do this already, then start, You never knew when you're going to take a note that could change your life. Any ideas, significant thoughts, important dates, times, addresses or anything that stands out to you, get it written down.

I'd found it. '7 habits of highly effective people' was written in the late 80's by Stephen R Covey who was basically a walking, talking brain and arguably one of the founders of modern personal development. In coaching and therapy circles pretty much everyone has read it at least once. This book introduced me to the idea of finding out what success actually means; beyond money, big houses, fast cars and fake tits. How family, relationships, being happy in your own skin and loving what you do are the real success. It also introduced me to the idea of exchanging bad habits for good ones, considering why people do what they do (especially when what they did makes them look like a dick) and gave me real tools that I could start using to change my life. After all, all this positive talk and woo woo thinking is great and everything but I like tactics and tools I can employ. Even now, this is what I like to give my coaching clients.

I listened to the book on my commute to and from work, sometimes taking the long route so I could get a few extra minutes in. I finished the book within a couple of weeks, immediately after finishing it the first time I listened to it a second time and started writing down important parts. After the second time of listening to it, I was obsessed with learning more. I found other books that covered the various topics in more detail. Things like managing your time effectively, stress management, how to make and maintain strong relationships with people and developing a positive mindset. Quickly I developed a daily routine in which I'd watch a motivational YouTube video before work, then listen to an audiobook on my way to work, making sure I noted down important parts of what I'd heard on my phone once I got to work and then read articles on the internet about all this stuff. I'd write everything down on my phone. I had no plan for them at the time but these notes would later become ideas for this book, content for other books, speeches for public speaking events and would form the foundation for how I coach my clients.

I began to see glimpses of emotion within myself again, something which I'd given up all hope of by this point. During one of my lowest points I found a really well written blog someone had done about depression and its effects. It spoke a lot about how the writer lost their emotions and after a long time of suffering, one day they were lying on the kitchen floor crying (yeah, this is a real thing with depression), after a while they noticed a single piece of dried sweetcorn underneath the fridge and for some unknown reason found it hysterically funny, they couldn't stop laughing at this lump of old sweetcorn and felt overwhelmed by the sudden rush of emotion and the joy of being able to feel again. I'd been looking for my bit of sweetcorn everywhere and no matter what I did, I couldn't find it and started to think the whole thing could be bullshit. I resigned myself to the fact that I might never feel again.

For a while I actually loved not feeling any emotion, I felt like it made me like one of those stoic, thousand yard stare action hero types you see in the movies. The type of character who could shoot a hundred bad guys, hold a new born baby or get shit-faced drunk at a New Years party and in every scenario, he showed all the emotion of someone who's had gone overboard with the Botox. I was a hard-nosed, tough talking, no nonsense bastard and nobody could bring me down.

Except I wasn't, I'd seen a lot of people get killed and it affected me in ways I never thought possible, I held my best mates new born baby and it killed me that I felt no attachment to it and whenever I got drunk I usually ended up having some massive anxiety attack and had to get out of the area before I started swinging my fists at anyone who got in my way out the door. Not only was I not the cold-hearted action hero type, things affected me way more than I was ready to admit, and if I was honest with myself, I didn't want to the distant type. You know why? Because in order to be really like the characters that Jason Statham and Arnold Schwarzenegger portray you would need to be a complete psychopath, lonely as fuck and probably dead a hundred times over. Life isn't like what you see in the movies, the sooner people realise that the sooner they can get on with their own **real** life. We need to stop living out this bullshit social media fantasy life while feeling miserable as fuck in the real world and take responsibility for our lives. For those who follow me on social media, this is why you'll see me post about the times when I'm not doing so good or things about me that I want to change. It's the real me, not a bullshit façade.

Within a couple of weeks, things started changing noticeably with my life. Things were better at home, Kel was happier, our relationship was more solid and I began taking better care of myself, my family and the house. I felt happier in myself and with my new-found non-arsehole approach to people I was making friends out in civvy street, simply by opening myself up to the possibility that they're a good person. One of the biggest surprises was how effective my new approach had been to work. I'd gone from clinging on to my job by my finger nails because I was so under-qualified and angry, to being praised and rewarded as the best performing engineer in my team and was setting my sights on working up to senior management, earn shit loads of money, work from home and be an 'exec' and I was on the right path to achieve this. Now this isn't meant to be 'Look how amazing I am!' because I'm really not. But it is meant to prove that if I can go from a total useless sack of shit that was so underqualified for a job that I really should have been fired after week one to the top performer in the company in the space of a couple of months, then anyone else can do the same. All it takes is the right mind-set, a willingness to learn and be willing to put the work in and you can change your life in a surprisingly short amount of time.

The single biggest change however was in how I viewed the events of the past. Having identified that I was playing the victim I decided to stop looking at my past and blaming everyone else and start looking at my future and consider the possibilities of what I could achieve. Through expanding my mind with books and personal development materials I worked out that I was actively sabotaging my recovery. I hated listening to certain songs because particular lines in the song reminded me of a painful memory. Seeing any military vehicle painted in desert camouflage made me feel like shit and that sudden and uncontrollable urge to cry that I'd had years ago would come. Also, I still remembered the dates and names of some of the guys I'd seen get hurt on tour. But what was I gaining by remembering those details? It only made me feel like shit and I was well aware that there were military vehicles out there, they're just vehicles and they didn't have to mean anything.

Now this isn't to say that certain things in media and in the world around us can't trigger certain memories and emotions. Of course they can and it's a completely natural thing. But if you're actively going out of your way to seek out these things (like trying to remember the names of the lads who got hurt) or create your own bullshit association with something (like pick out a single line from a song to create a certain association) then you're just fucking yourself over. It's a choice you're making to create a negative association that isn't necessary or helpful. It wasn't protecting me from anything, it didn't benefit me in any way; it only held me back.

For example, take 'Say something' by a band called 'A great big world'. A beautiful song in its own right. One line in the chorus of that song says 'I'm sorry that I couldn't get to you', that line tore me up inside because I thought about not being able to get to the guys I saw get hit in Afghan. But the song isn't about that; it's about the breakdown of a relationship and it's one line in a whole song. So why did it affect me so much? Because I made that decision that it should, rather than just enjoy the song for what it is. One day I made the conscious decision to stop being a silly twat and just enjoy the song and with a bit of practice, that's exactly what I did.

I'm rambling a bit here but that's because the point is an important one.

While we may not choose what life throws at us. We get to choose what we think and feel about the things around us. We create associations in our own mind and we can choose to be a victim or to be the champion of our own minds.

I feel like I could stop there but fuck it, I'm going to drive this point home. When it comes to certain things in life, we all need to get professional help (mental health issues or an addiction for example) and that's absolutely fine, we all need help with something. But that isn't to say that you're completely in that person's hands and you have no control. If you can take back even the smallest amount of control then you're onto a winner. Unhappy about your weight? You can sit and feel shit about it, maybe eat some cake. Or go out for a 5-minute jog. Unhappy with your job? Identify something you can change to improve your situation, maybe chat to your boss about what can be changed to improve things or just look for a new job. In bed feeling like shit because your depression is beating the shit out of you? Have a shower, throw on some clothes and make your bed. An achievement, however small, is still an achievement. When those dark clouds start to gather, they will try to convince you that you have no control over this and you're in for the ride now. But they're lying to you. You do have a choice in this.

The only person in charge of you, is you.

Chapter 21

'Oh, shiny shiny!'

When talking to high ranking officers SAC White must only say things from the pre-agreed list

So, things were going well. Home and work life were both doing great. I wasn't having any more therapy, I was coming off my meds, and the last few months of my service with the military I was earning 2 payslips; one from the MOD and one from my job in IT. I was fecking minted (which lasted all of 3 months)!

I was gradually learning how to overcome or learn to live with the remaining effects of my PTSD and felt positive about the future. One of the biggest left-overs from my dark times was anxiety. Before any of this stuff had started, I was more than happy in crowded places, happy to socialize and loved getting pissed. But now I felt seriously uncomfortable in crowds, although I could meet new people and hold a conversation it was only if I really had to. Additionally, booze made my anxiety symptoms 10 times worse. In my younger years I was a big drinker, loved getting off my face and doing stupid shit. Gradually this evolved into enjoying a few quiet pints down the pub, get a bit pissed and grab a kebab on the way home. These days however, I couldn't drink any more than 1 pint before things started going wrong. On the second pint I noticed that I became hyper aware of everything around me, I started doing that profiling thing again and I could feel my heart beating. If I didn't stop drinking and go somewhere quiet things would get worse; I got agitated, I'd start snapping at people and would start checking for exits and points for effective cover because in my mind, I was playing out scenarios of attacks or emergencies such as explosions or fire. At this point I either had to leave now or I'd start reverting to my arsehole stage, talking to everyone with a massive sense of urgency. It was as if I was barking orders and if they didn't follow then life was at risk.

After a few incidents of this happening I decided it wasn't worth drinking and completely packed it in. Over the next year or so I had a few test-runs of drinking more than 2 drinks to see if things had eased off. It never did, so eventually I packed it in. These days I don't drink more than 1 beer every couple of weeks. To be honest I don't miss it and it saves me a fortune when going out. The downside of this is I've learnt that alcohol turns anyone into an annoying wanker.

The other element was an interesting one. My brain was off-the-rails bat shit crazy. Now, I don't mean crazy in the same ways as you've been reading about in the previous chapters, I mean my brain just never stopped, it was hyper-active all the time. I would constantly be thinking of new (usually dumb) inventions, business ideas; ways that my current employer could expand their business or start my own business. Within a month at my first job I had thought up, researched, written a 4-page proposal and pitched it to the management for a new area for the business to move into. I was thinking of book ideas, websites, apps, new hobbies, basically whatever little nugget of something I found, my head would grab hold and run with it.

This, accompanied with my obsession for success and drive for achievement meant that I never stopped. From the minute I woke up to the minute I collapsed into my bed because I was fucking knackered, I was on the go and couldn't settle for more than a few minutes.

This was a double-edged sword. On one side, it kept me distracted from anything that happened in the past and kept me looking to the future, it helped me feel productive, it fed my need for progress and achievement and helped me stand out from everyone else in work. On the other hand, it drove Kel crazy and I had so much going on I usually ended up achieving very few of the ideas I came up with. I even planned on starting an online store in which I'd buy cheap crap from China and sell it on for a profit. That died when I realised that I didn't have a clue what I was doing. A few times a week I'd get home from work, excitedly tell Kel about my next big idea that would make us shit loads of money. She'd roll her eyes but still begrudgingly support me. I'd obsessively research the idea because I was **definitely** going to do it and then sack it off when I worked out that it was stupid.

I needed to find an outlet for my bat-shit crazy head. Something that I enjoyed, something that I was good at, something that ideally would make money and keep me on the right side of the law. It took a couple of chance conversations with guys from my job in IT to help me work it out.

My new passion for positive mind-set, success, using habits and tactics to help me get my shit together, both personally and professionally was not only great for me personally, but I wanted to share it with other people. The more I looked around the more I saw people just floating through life, hating their job or complaining that some aspect of their life was shit and they felt stuck. I could identify where they were coming from but knew that if they knew how they could grab life by the bollocks (or ovaries) they could get their shit together. I never tried to ram any of this stuff down their throat, but people started to notice my positive attitude and how I managed to stay calm when everything went wrong around us (something that happens frequently in IT).

A colleague at work pulled me aside one day and asked for a chat; they had seen me post about my mental health issues on Facebook, being open about what was going on and trying to do my part to get rid of the stigma. She wanted to tell me about her issues with mental health and the problems in her personal life and she wanted some advice. I didn't give her the advice she wanted because I haven't got the answers to her problems, but I was able to give her some pretty solid tips and tricks for getting started on getting herself squared away. Shortly after this one of the guys on my team asked me for advice because he was having a hard time keeping up with the amount of work being asked of him. Again, we had a sit down and just talked about what was going on with him and worked out a plan to make things easier for him.

Both of these chats were quick 10-minute conversations, neither of them had earth-shattering outcomes but both people found a lot of benefit in just venting off their issues and having someone show them a different point of view or way they could tackle what was going on. Not only that but it made me realise something had happened since those early days of first getting into civvy street; I had gone from someone who actively disliked the majority of the human population (and wasn't discreet about it) to someone who really enjoyed speaking to people and helping them with shit in their lives. This also had a knock-on realisation. Despite the fact I was getting pretty good with the whole IT side of things; it didn't excite me, I wasn't bothered about a career in IT or a career in management. The corporate world suffered from almost as much bullshit as the military world, and most people were fucking miserable in this environment.

Some mornings I would sit in my car and watch people walk into the shared office block I worked from. Nobody was smiling, nobody looked happy to be there. In fact, many of them looked stressed as balls. I didn't want this for myself, I didn't want to repeat this every week day for the next 40 years so I could earn enough to enjoy my retirement, only be too knackered to enjoy the things I'd been working to enjoy. If this is OK for you then I'm genuinely happy for you, more power to you. But this wasn't for me and this wasn't my idea of success. My version of success is freedom, both financial and with my time, spending quality time with my family, being able to do and have the things we want and also to be at the top of my game in whatever I did.

What I did want was to help the people who were looking miserable and stressed walking into work every morning; to find something that didn't make them stressed or miserable. Whether that's a new way of doing their job or even a new job. Maybe improve their home life, relationship, bank account, whatever it was that was causing them to feel the way they did. But what kind of person does this? Who just rocks up in someone's life and goes 'Hey, that shitty thing you have going on there? Yeah, I can make that not shitty! Just pay me and I'll show you how!' (This by the way, is the single worst ever description of what coaching is).

I had an idea (which in my head is nothing new), but this time it felt different to the previous bullshit I'd conjured up. It wasn't just some scheme to make some extra cash or a half-baked idea that might or might not work. This felt real, and although I hadn't realised it previously, I'd already been putting in the ground work for this concept for months with all my personal development and self-help work I'd been doing. Not only that, but I'd already done in my own life what I wanted to help others to do. To overcome whatever obstacles (no matter how shitty) were in the way and improve their life. I wasn't a rich man, and I was under no illusion that I was some mega-talented self-help guru (spoiler alert: most of these guys are full of shit and trying to sell sand in the desert by the way). I was a happy man, I'd turned failure into success, I had a great home life and I'd built something from nothing. This is what I wanted to do.

That's all great but I still had no idea what it was even called or how I could turn it into a business. So, I set about finding out in typical me fashion, googling the shit out of it and asking everyone I could find if they knew what I was on about. After a few funny looks and rude 'I have no idea now get out of my house you strange man!' replies, a few folks came back with the answer. Life coaching. I'd heard of this term before but never put any thought into it because it was something I'd always dismiss as woo-woo snake oil bullshit. But the more I looked into this the more it matched up with my idea. Life coaching, in its simplest form, is helping someone who hasn't been able to achieve something in their life, whatever it is. With coaching, people can work out what is holding them back and once they work this out, they can work out how to overcome whatever and move on to achieve their goal. Now that's pretty vague because it's a very high-level overview of life coaching. That's because there are loads of different flavours and types of coaches, all work differently, have different niches and often use different approaches. This slotted in perfectly to what I wanted to do. Why? Because I'd been to the bottom of the barrel in life, I knew that there was nothing that couldn't be overcome. Over the last 6 years I'd managed to get myself from a quivering mess on the floor to someone who was smashing it at life. Another benefit of using my experience to help others was the fact that there was nothing that anyone could tell me that would shock me because chances are, I'd done it or thought worse. I knew I didn't want to be one of these coach types who stands on the side like a cheer leader, shouting encouragement but doing fuck all to actual help. I wanted to be the type of coach that would call someone out on their bullshit, help them get their head out their arse, get shit done and achieve major success.

I had identified a problem (the miserable people walking into work) and the solution (coaching). What I needed now was a method of how to do it. I knew that I had a solid foundation in the coaching and success mind-set, but I wasn't arrogant enough to think that I could just start coaching, help loads of people change their lives and earn loads of money doing it. I had to get some training in how to be a coach; back to Google I went. There are loads of coaching training providers out there and they range from the sublime to the fucking horrendous. Some of them asked for 25 quid for a 6-part online video course which will turn you into a super coach, others asked for £10k to attend a month-long retreat in the mountains. I even found one who asked for £6k to turn you into a coach by sending you a bunch of PowerPoint presentations and even promised that you would earn £5000 in your first month of coaching. Anyone who has ever sat through a training course that uses PowerPoint will know the only thing you earn is a sore arse and a large void where your will to live once was.

Eventually I found a coach training provider that seemed to fit the mould. Animas Coaching is based in the UK, the feedback was mega, and they were completely bullshit free. None of this 'train with us and you'll be minted!' shite and no PowerPoint shite either. I won't bore you with the details of the course. The actual content of the course was fucking brilliant and worth every penny I paid for it but to properly do it justice would require a complete second book. (Maybe that's something for the future, who knows?).

What I rapidly found out though was that coaching wasn't about 'Do this and it'll be awesome'. In fact, there's very little of that involved. A decent coach spends far more time listening than talking. It's about finding out what's going on for the person, then digging down to find out where the root of their problems are, over the course of our time together. Eventually when we've dug down to the bottom of their barrel (see what I did there!?) we can focus on their future and how they can change things in their life to get their shit together. That makes it sound a bit like therapy, it's not. Therapy focuses much more on a person's history and dealing with what has happened. Coaching looks a little bit at someone's history but focuses heavily on building their future. It's heavily based in psychology and the idea is to help a person see what they couldn't see before so they've got a much better understanding of a situation. This usually helps them find a solution or see a new path they couldn't see before. Mix that in with giving them tools in personal effectiveness, habits, time management and generally being awesome and you're onto a winner.

I loved Animas and what they do, it is genuinely brilliant. But for me doing this course and passing it felt a bit like passing a driving test. Animas had built on the foundation skills I developed when I moves across into civvy street. As time went on and I got better at coaching I felt like I wanted to create my own method of coaching. It wasn't until I passed the tests that I was able to break free from any rules or methods that didn't sit right with me, take the stuff that did work for me and adapt it with my existing style and start coaching in my own way. Coaching has allowed me to focus my mind; rather than trying to do 15 different things at once, I can focus on one thing and do it well. When I'm coaching someone it's the only time my mind is settled. I'm 100% present in the moment with that person. Nothing else matters in the world other than helping them get their shit together. Having a job where, when I'm doing it, I'm completely relaxed and at ease and I get to help someone get from 'I have no idea how I'm going to do this' to 'Holy shit I did that, and so much more!', is the best fucking job in the world.

Chapter 22

So, what now?

SAC White must not stuff his beret down his pants and proposition people to a night with 'Lord Longrod Von Hugendong'

Looking back over the last decade, from first joining the military, when I was young and clueless. To my time in Afghan, the Olympics, my early symptoms of minor depression and PTSD, eventually leading to a full-blown mental health crisis. I can pick out points that were little sign posts, pointing me towards where I am today. Small dots on a piece of paper, that when joined together, create a map which leads me to where I am now. The fact I joined the RAF and not the Army, the fact I got injured in basic training meaning that I deployed when I did and where I did, with the people I did. Meeting Kel on that cruise ship, the person who would later go on to save my life and change my life. What if I hadn't of been training for that half marathon, fucked my knee up and met that physio who would suggest I read '7 habits of highly effective people'. The list of events goes on and on. Almost every week now, I meet someone new who opens up a new possibility in my life which is leading to the scope of my business growing faster than I'd ever imagined.

Some of these sign posts were great things; meeting Kel and getting Meg for example. Others were the hardest days I've ever had and at the time seemed like a shit smeared sandwich of suffering, like sitting in a puddle of my own piss or contemplating my own suicide. Whatever they were at the time they've all had a part to play in creating that road map of my life where now I'm here, sat at my laptop at 2am in the morning because my mind is having one of its batshit moments and I can't sleep. But I'm happy, the happiest I've ever been, I have THE best fucking job in the world where I get paid to help people change their lives. I've helped people double the size of their business, I've helped people make it through a messy divorce and come out the other side happy, and others have left a career they hated and moved on to do something that they love so much that they don't see it as work. I have THE best wife in the world, and even though she's a Brummie and rarely shuts up I couldn't imagine life without her. Not to mention THE cutest dog in the world who is a big part of the reason I'm still here.

From the day that welfare Sergeant walked out of the house with my ID in hand I never did hear another word from the MOD. Even on my discharge date. I've spoken to many veterans, many of whom were medically discharged for various reasons, some of them with life changing injuries. Not one of them have heard a whisper from the MOD since they left, not a 'How's things?' or 'Could you do with any help?'. I've got my own thoughts on this, but I'll allow you to draw your own conclusions.

Today, my health is good. I'm 90% symptom free from depression and PTSD, to the point where I doubt that I could be diagnosed with PTSD; which I guess means that I've beaten it. I still get the odd symptom now and then, mainly anxiety in crowds or I'll be forced to deal with the death of someone. For the most part, I have my ability to feel emotions again and I still find physical closeness a challenge but I'm working on these. I find the whole remembrance period in November really tough going.

Due to the nature of PTSD and depression, and every now and then something will pop up which will start those dark clouds gathering again. I'll start feeling anxious, profiling people, becoming hyper-aware of my surroundings or start thinking of dead people. I've given my PTSD and anxiety type thoughts a name; Kevin. So that when it pipes up, I can just say 'Shut the fuck up Kevin' which takes the power away from it. I remind myself that there's no evidence that anyone is in danger and that most people are inherently good. If I feel my depression creeping back, I make a point of picking one small thing for that day to achieve. It can be anything from making the bed to washing the dishes. Any small win so I feel like I've achieved something. Sometimes I'll even force myself to smile or laugh; I feel fucking stupid doing it, but it helps get those endorphins going. I do everything in my power to keep those clouds at bay. Depression takes the fight out of you, so I do the opposite; I fight harder than ever. If one day they do take control, I know that there's help out there and I can beat it.

Recently a good friend of mine and Kels passed away due to leukaemia, she had been ill for a over a decade, but a chest infection prompted a series of complications which finished her off. As we sat by the side of her bed, after they had stopped any treatment and were waiting for nature to take its course. Facing death at such a close proximity caused those little PTSD demon bastards to come back to haunt me; things like memories of people dying, visions of death, horrific thoughts of physically hurting everyone sat around that bed and the nurses in the hospital. By this point I'd built up a pretty good resistance to this sort of shit and have my own little tool kit I can use to fight off this type of thing, but this was relentless. Every time I fought off one horrific thought my mind would conjure up another to try and drag me down again. Eventually I stepped away to take some time to sort my head out. I walked for a while through the hallways, eventually settling on a bench off to the side near the entrance to the hospital. As I sat there trying to calm the shit storm kicking off in my head I looked up and saw a picture on the wall. It was a picture of a MERT team, Chinook helicopter behind them, kicking up a shit load of sand. The medics were tending to a Brit soldier who looked like he'd taken a round to the chest. Now it felt like the universe was joining forces with my head, trying to suck me back in. I just laughed, said "Oh fuck off" and walked away.

That's the thing with PTSD, some people say that you can never life a normal life with PTSD. That's bullshit, you can. Though some guys may never be able to recover to the extent that I have. We just need to be aware that those little pesky demon wankers are still there, what happened in your life happened, there's no changing that and sometimes they will try to drag you back down to that place again. **FUCK THAT.** You've fought too hard and come too far to let that happen, so when it does, fight that shit with everything you've got because you're stronger than those demons.

Remember back at the start when I said that PTSD has taken a lot of my memories? Yeah, that's something I'll probably be working on for the rest of my life. Recently I had a conversation with my mum, it was probably one of the toughest conversations I'd ever had. I told her that I never felt like we'd been close or even got on that well. I said that I wanted to put all that behind us and be a closer family. I always thought that this was common knowledge in the family, so I was surprised when she didn't know what I was taking about. Turns out that I had a great relationship with my family, and we were always close. I'd just lost loads of those memories that you would associate with a good childhood. Huge chunks of time, just gone. It's definitely one of the more fucked up symptoms of PTSD. I'm gradually piecing together those years with the help of my family.

So, what now? Well I've got a good thing going here but I'm not going to be resting on my laurels. I'm going to continue coaching. I'm also getting into public speaking, so I can use what happened to me to educate others on mental health, how to get through those shit times and how to build your best life; building on that image of success I discovered after I left the RAF and help others achieve their own success.

And would I change anything? Not really. Yeah going through all of that stuff was properly shit, like really bad diarrhoea shit. But it's got me where I am today, and where I am today is awesome, so no, I don't regret it. Plus, I know that I've been to the very bottom of my barrel and come out the other side. So, when life does start going south again, I know that however bad it gets, I know things will improve again and I can come out the other side. There are a couple of things I wish I hadn't of done. Like trying to break that couple up over a stupid Facebook disagreement and trying to run that guy over. But that's really about it. I don't even regret putting my wife through hell for all those years. I know that sounds odd, but it's made us stronger as individuals and as a couple. And it's given us the confidence that we can take what life throws at us and stick it out.

Regret feels pointless to me; it achieves nothing other than to keep us looking back to the past. We usually end up missing what's there in the present and what's possible in the future. Also, what we have done in our lives previously, lines us up for our future lives. Without my time in the military and getting seriously mentally fucked up I wouldn't be where I am today. And I love where I am today.

Aside from overcoming my issues with mental health, one of the best things I did was take action to improve my life. I noticed that I was coasting through life, waking up as late as my commute to work would allow, going to work, finishing and getting home and then wait until I did the same the next day. Not only is it boring as fuck but it's a complete waste of potential. I audited my day from start to finish, what I was doing, at what time and for how long and what I achieved. I noticed where I had slots of wasted time and found ways to make better use of it. Gradually my daily schedule grew from eat, sleep, work, repeat to a full and rich day of achievements and growth. Take my morning routine for example. Before I would wake up at 8am, get ready and go to work. Now I'm up at 6 am, and make the bed, I'll go for a run or get some gym time in, get home and take the dog out for a walk. Do 15 minutes housework, have breakfast, get myself showered and ready and then spend 20-30 minutes relaxing, usually with one of those motivational YouTube videos, meditating or just watching some shite TV to get my mind settled before starting work, I'll also listen to a non-fiction audio book on my commute.

This means that by the time I start work I've already accomplished 4 or 5 small tasks, given myself a quick shot of motivation, given myself chance to relax so I'm fresh for work and gained a small piece of knowledge. This type of rigid structure might sound soul destroying to some but for me it's turned me from someone wasting their time and potential to someone who consistently achieves their goals and enjoys their free time without worrying about stuff I haven't done. I'm never bored, and I know that when I do sit in front of the TV at the end of the day, I've earnt it.

And for you reading this? Well, you've got a choice. If you're one of those people who walks into work every day wishing they were somewhere different, miserable, stressed and pissed off because your life didn't work out the way you planned. You can choose to continue in the same way, allowing life to feed you shit sandwiches or you can choose to change. If you open yourself up to the possibility that your situation can get better, whether it's your health, finances or personal circumstances then you open yourself up to a whole new life. Join the dots of your life and look at where the map takes you. You're in control of your own destiny, none of this 'fate' or 'the universe has a plan' bullshit, it's down to you. Audit your own life, how do you spend your time? What do you achieve in your days? If you're not happy with it then take steps to change it. If some overweight bloke in his 30's who once sat in a puddle of his own piss thinking of the best way to kill himself can achieve his dreams, then surely you can?

It's time to climb out from your barrel.

Afterword

I wanted to include some lessons that I learned from suffering with massive mental health issues. Additionally, I wanted to give lessons from the point of view of a veteran and a civilian since leaving the military because both mental health and leaving the military can be really shit times and I remember looking for advice everywhere about how to make things easier. Don't take these as gospel, they're just things that I thought up and have served me well.

If you're going through a hard time due to mental health issues

This section in which I impart my 'wisdom' is all about mental health. For me this is the most important part because anyone can talk about a veteran leaving the forces and there's no taboo around it. But when it comes to mental health, it's like talking about sex toys; loads of people have them but nobody talks about it openly. But the real kicker is that talking openly about it is exactly what's needed if we're going to reduce the number of people who end up taking their own life or living a life of suffering.

Talk. Talk. Talk

Early on in my troubles with mental health difficulties, I made a point to talk openly about my problems with my head, I tried to talk about it like someone would talk about breaking a leg or getting ill in some other less taboo way. Talking openly about what was going on probably saved my life. It meant that I didn't need to hide what was going on, make up stories about why I was taking time off work or why I would sometimes sit staring into the void or lose my temper over nothing. Over the years I'd had figures of authority tell me that if I did need anything or if I had to step out of the office for a bit I could, and while I'd lost a lot of friends along the way (some through them not being interested in me, others through me being a cock), those I had kept were firm friends and always there if I needed anything. But none of these people would have been there if I hadn't of told them what was going on. It gave me the freedom to reply with 'I feel like shit' when someone asked how I was rather than make up some bullshit about being fine or pretending to have a hangover to explain away why I looked like shit or cancelled a night out last minute.

For a lot of people, talking to anyone about their mental health feels like a huge hurdle because of a fear of being judged, feeling shame, looking weak or even losing their job. Look, any of this stuff might happen, I won't lie to you. I did feel shame, I felt like a fraud, eventually (but only after things got mega serious) I lost my job and I was judged by my management. But none of this stuff was nearly anywhere near as bad as if I hadn't of spoken to anyone about what was going on. You know how I know? Because if I didn't have anyone to speak to, I guarantee you that I'd be dead now.

Now I appreciate that talking about your mental health so openly may feel like a step too far. That's not what I'm suggesting. What I am suggesting is to speak to just one person about what's going on for you, nobody in particular, just choose one person and talk to them. That conversation will probably change your life.

Strap in

Having a mental illness isn't plain sailing. Depression isn't one continuous string of feeling like shit, OCD isn't being obsessive of every thought, every hour of every day. PTSD isn't being constantly angry, easily startled, flashbacks etc every day. It's more like a roller coaster where you can't see what's in front of you. You'll have times where the symptoms seem to ease off and life gets easier. When this happens enjoy it, try to recognise if something in particular got you there, take note of it and add it to your tool kit. Don't however, get complacent with your treatment and meds. It's easy to be feeling pretty good and think you're sorted. Hell, even my docs made that mistake more than once.

You may genuinely be sorted, but if you haven't been tackling your issues with treatment and medication then there's a chance that things might go downhill again. When this happens strap in for the ride, you don't know how deep it's going to go and you don't know how long it's going to last for. What you do need to remember however, is that you will eventually come back up again. So, strap in and prepare to ride it out. This leads me nicely onto my next lesson.

Fight

As I've established already in this book, mental illness has a habit of beating the shit out of you. It will do its very best to make you feel worthless, useless, helpless and turn you into a prisoner of your own mind. But it's lying to you, you're not any of those things. In fact, if you've got a mental health issue, you're not a prisoner or a victim, you're a tough mother fucker. The reason being, your worst enemy is right on top of you 24 hours a day, 7 days a week. This enemy knows exactly what your weaknesses are, what makes you tick. It's an expert at playing mind games and it's also the biggest arsehole you will ever know. Remember, you're still here, still fighting every day, even when things feel hopeless.

So, whatever you're going through keep up the fight, it doesn't matter how low you are, what's going on around you or what's happened in the past. Nothing lasts forever which means that this shit will pass. It could be tomorrow, next week, next month or a year down the line. It will pass though; you can, and will, beat this. Keep up with the treatment and meds, find your own tools that help you and though you may not realise it. You have people to support you around you, **use them**.

At the start of an episode of a mental illness you still have a chance to fight it before you go too far down into the rabbit hole. When you notice those dark clouds forming you may not feel like it, but you have a choice, you can either let the clouds gather and drag you down to those familiar depths. Or you can choose to say 'nah fuck this!' and fight it. You can do small things like take a shower, text a loved one, go for a walk, sometimes this is all that is needed to remind yourself that this isn't permanent. The real kicker is that when you start feeling the dark clouds forming, you won't feel like doing any of this. That's because your mental illness is lying to you, trying to convince you that you have no control over this. Tell that little voice to piss off, at this point, you're still in control and you still have a chance to help yourself.

However, if you're in the same position I was when I was at my lowest point; feeling completely worthless, hopeless and lost. Please remember this, you will feel emotions again, you will laugh again, you will love again, you will have amazing sex again, you will be successful at something again, you will have friends again, you will be in control again, you will enjoy a warm bath again. Your head is lying to you, there is hope, this will pass, you can do this. You only need to strap in and keep fighting a bit longer because the light is there, right behind those dark clouds.

Tips for veterans

Leaving the military and having to find your way in civilian life is tough going. I served for 9 years and did comparatively very little in my time in service and even I found it difficult. I can't imagine what it's like for the guys who have done 20+ years and multiple tours. Making the jump is scary but it's inevitable, it's going to happen at some point.

A lot of the work I do in coaching is helping veterans make this leap, usually at a pretty deep level. We won't go anywhere near that deep here. The biggest factor is fear of the unknown and trying to approach civvy life but in a military manner. Below I've included some tips for making the transition into civvy street a bit easier.

Give yourself a break

OK, so this one may be a little rich coming from me seeing as I went into civvy life full on and tried to take over the world in my first few weeks. That's because I had found something that distracted me from my mental health issues and it excited the shit out of me.

You've just spent X amount of years dealing with constant bullshit, earning yourself arthritis and back problems and in a life that can go from 0 to 100 in the blink of an eye. When you get out allow yourself to take a bit of time to regroup and relax, you've earned it.

When you do start to get going, particularly with a new job give yourself time to learn the ropes. You may have been a high flyer in your unit but you may be the bottom of the pile now. That's OK, you've got a lot to learn. Some of the stuff you need to learn will seem basic to your civvy counterparts. Don't be afraid to ask and learn. Have conversations with as many people as you can, open doors and create opportunities.

Get over yourself

Now this one might rub some folks up the wrong way but it's vital. So many forces veterans out there come across like entitled pricks because they served in the forces. Some even talk down to civilians just because they didn't serve. You need to put that shit to bed **NOW**. What you did in the military was great, I'm sure you got up to some impressive shit, I'm sure you were really fucking good at what you did and yes you will probably have skills and attributes that are valuable and more highly honed than many civvy's out there. This makes you better than precisely no-one.

Civvy's do some mega impressive stuff as well, they'll have skills that make you look like a 6-year-old and they can teach you a lot. When you were in service you were probably told that Civvy's are all lazy, entitled, work shy cocks. Well, some of them are, but only about the same proportion as you saw in the military. Don't add to that demographic by thinking you're better than anyone else because of your service.

This isn't to say you can't share some stories from your past life, just don't be a pompous dick about it. More on this in the next lesson but for now follow this simple tip: **Don't be a cock**.

Share your story, within reason

Many civvy's do find stories about your service interesting as it's a world many of them don't get much exposure to. Also, the military do get up to some interesting and funny shit (for example almost shooting a guy for taking a crap) but when a veteran goes on and on about their time in service, they become a one trick pony. Don't close yourself up to creating interesting stories in your new civilian life by living in your old military life. So, tell your story but just make sure it's:

A. **True** – Don't make up bullshit. Civvy's can usually spot it and eventually a veteran will catch you out

B. **Interesting** – Telling someone how it was really hot in Afghan is a bit like telling people that water is wet. Like anything else, if you're story is shit nobody will be interested

C. **Not the same old shit** – Despite what you think, there's more to life than your time in the military and even an interesting story, once told, becomes old news. Learn to listen more than you talk, you'll learn a lot.

Use your skills

In most civilian jobs there's not much requirement to accurately shoot a weapon at 100 yards, set up a satellite dish in the middle of the desert or do parade drill. But you do have some incredibly valuable skills and qualities that civilian employers love and are inherent with time spent in the military like:

- Time management
- 'Get shit done' mentality
- Respect
- Cheerfulness when the shit hits the fan
- Discipline
- Attention to detail

I could go on for ages. My point is that although you may not know it, the military gave you some incredibly valuable transferrable skills for civilian life. Use them and play up to them. People will notice and appreciate it.

Stupid questions

You will get asked some really dumb questions. Sometimes it's genuine naivety and other times they're being a dick. It can be difficult when people ask you this shit and it's up to you how you deal with it. All I would say is don't make yourself out to be a bigger dick than the person that asked it in the first place.

Personally, when someone asks me 'Have you ever killed anyone?' I like to reply "Yes, 8 people. None of them for work though, it's more of a hobby" and walk away calmly. I'll cover more on the stupid questions side later on but as a veteran your only takeaway is try to take it in good humour and don't be a dick if someone asks you one. Unless they're genuinely trying to wind you up, in which case, yeah, have some fun!

Jargon

We all know the forces have their own word for pretty much everything, it works pretty well and it's funny as fuck. Usually it only works while you're around other forces people. Most (not all) civvy's have no idea what 'gopping' (which means disgusting) is, or a 'hot wet' (a hot drink). 'hoofing' will make them think you're a fan of horses rather than saying something is brilliant and 'stand by' (meaning to wait) will have them standing still while looking at you funny. My point is, give it a rest a bit. Don't get me wrong, sometimes I still find myself using military slang for a few things but if nobody knows what you're on about because you're talking like you're back on your unit you won't make friends quickly. Having said that when you do meet another veteran it's great to be able to talk properly again.

Tips for civilians

OK so above I wrote about tips for veterans coming into civilian life, but I think it's just as important for people who have never served to know how to make a veteran's transition as easy as possible. It's important to understand that they've just come from a world in its own bubble. It's got its own communities, its own laws, jobs you will never see anywhere else and in many cases its own dialect and it's very difficult to get sacked from that job. What a veteran got away with for the past x amount of years might not wash in civvy street. Leaving their service life is a big shock to the system for them, and that's before we even touch on the subject of mental health issues often associated with the forces, such as PTSD. So, here's a few tips to make their lives a little easier so you can help them to help you.

Be patient

As I mentioned above this is a big change for anyone leaving the forces. When I first made the jump, I didn't know what a company director was, I didn't know that civvy's don't talk about what they earn and I didn't know that customers pay for everything, there's no such thing as favours for a packet of Hob Nobs or a crate of beer. Stuff that is basic to a civilian might be new for them. Give them plenty of time to settle in and learn the ropes. By the way, in case you're wondering, Hob Nobs and beer is common currency for favours in the forces.

Questions

If you're not familiar with the military world or you're a bit of a military geek; always wanting to get the inside scoop it's normal that you might want to ask questions. I've been asked all sorts since I left in 2017. Some of it was perfectly reasonable, other stuff was properly stupid. So, let's start with the elephant in the room. 'Have you ever killed anyone?'. If you don't know that this is a fucking stupid question, then you must have difficulty understanding basic human emotions. In case you have the emotional intelligence of a toddler, let me spell it out for you.

It's actually much rarer than you think that people in the forces do kill someone, of course it does happen but it's not like every soldier who was directly involved in combat operations in some shitty part of the world has killed a person, far from it. There's no official statistic for this because the results are massively skewed because most enemy deaths are not the result of someone pointing the weapon and pulling the trigger, there's usually a team of people working on a weapon system backed up by hundreds more people that made it possible to make the kill.

For the sake of argument, let's say someone pointed the weapon, pulled the trigger and killed the enemy. The person who did that is likely acutely aware that the person they killed had a family, their family maybe even saw them die. The person they shot may have not wanted to act as the enemy but were put in a position where they had no choice. Maybe the person who pulled the trigger questions whether or not the other guy was in fact an imminent threat to life and that question crosses their mind every day. This shit is **never** clear cut. By asking them this question you're just bringing all of that to the forefront of their mind again and bringing up whatever issues that they may have put to bed.

On the other side of the coin, let's say they haven't killed anyone. You may be thinking 'well, so what?' well not quite. Personally, I was racked with guilt for years because I didn't kill anyone on my tour. I know that may not make much sense but remember, I watched a lot of our guys get seriously injured or killed and the fact that I couldn't do anything proved to be an obsession for me. I know that looking back if I had of killed an insurgent it probably would have just fucked me up more but at the time it's all I thought about for ages and I thought about the prospect of it at an unhealthy level. Not anymore, but in the early days when people asked me this question it made me feel like shit because I felt like I should have killed someone.

War is a really shitty thing, and horrific things happen to people, as I mentioned in an earlier chapter. The fact that you're not told all of the details is completely intentional, because sometimes ignorance really is bliss.

My point is, just be mindful of what you're asking, do you really want to know the answer and why do you want to know it?

Be understanding

Veterans have a very unique sense of humour; they have developed the ability to crack a joke even in the darkest times. It's how the military deals with the fucked-up stuff they're exposed to. This leads to what can seem a pretty dark and twisted sense of humour to people who aren't from that world. It's one of the things I worried about when I left, what's acceptable and what's not? If a veteran says something that offends you, you have every right to tell them but just take a second to think, was it intended to offend? Or are they just trying to join in and

lighten the mood? Chances are it's the latter. Try to be understanding of their approach to things and their humour. I've been pulled up on what I considered to be really tame banter before because everyone else thought it was fucking brutal.

Well, that's it. Thanks for sticking with me through 55,000+ words of rambling. Hopefully you have enjoyed it and found some value in it. If you've got any questions or would like to work with me then please come see me at www.imperiumlifecoaching.com or drop me a message at pete@imperiumlifecoaching.com.

Printed in Great Britain
by Amazon